The
ALASKA CRUISE
HANDBOOK

A MILE BY MILE
GUIDE

The
ALASKA CRUISE
HANDBOOK

A MILE BY MILE

GUIDE

BY JOE UPTON

Coastal Publishing
Bainbridge Island, WA

The maps in this book are not to be used for navigation.

2012 Edition

Coastal Publishing
15166 Skogen Lane, Bainbridge Island, WA. 98110

Illustrations by Russ Burtner
Maps by Joe Upton

Photographs by Joe Upton unless noted with the following abbreviations:
AMNH - American Museum of Natural History, New York
BCARS - British Columbia Archives and Records Service.
BCRM- British Columbia Royal Museum.
CRMM - Columbia River Maritime Museum, Astoria, Oregon
MOHAI - Museum of History and Industry, Seattle.
SFM - San Francisco Maritime Museum.
THS - Tongass Historical Society, Ketchikan, Alaska.
UAF - University of Alaska, Fairbanks
UW - University of Washington Special Collections.
WAT - Whatcom County (WA) Museum of History and Art

ISBN 978-0-9794915-6-6 (Ship Cover Edition)
ISBN 978-0-9794915-7-3 (Iceberg Cover Edition)

For
John Enge,
1915 - 2010
Fisherman,
Canneryman,
Friend.

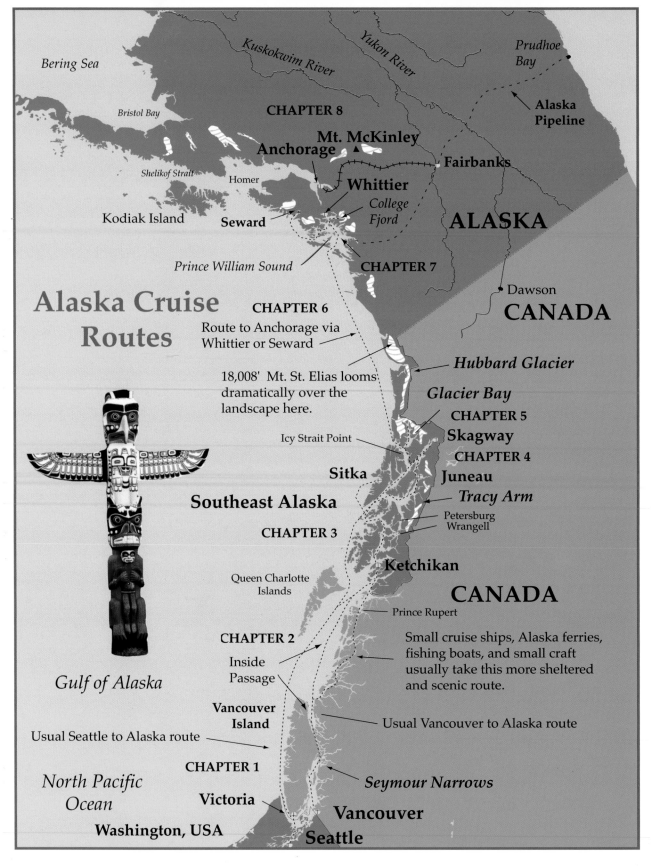

Kuskokwim River

Yukon River

Bering Sea

Prudhoe
Bay

CHAPTER 8

Alaska
Pipeline

Bristol Bay

Mt. McKinley
Anchorage ▲

Fairbanks

Shelikof Strait

Homer

Whittier

College
Fjord

ALASKA

Kodiak Island

Seward

Prince William Sound

CHAPTER 7

Dawson

CANADA

Alaska Cruise
Routes

CHAPTER 6
Route to Anchorage via
Whittier or Seward

Hubbard Glacier

18,008' Mt. St. Elias looms
dramatically over the
landscape here.

Glacier Bay
CHAPTER 5
Skagway

Icy Strait Point

CHAPTER 4
Juneau

Sitka

Tracy Arm

Southeast Alaska

Petersburg
Wrangell

CHAPTER 3

Ketchikan

Queen Charlotte
Islands

CANADA

Prince Rupert

Small cruise ships, Alaska ferries,
fishing boats, and small craft
usually take this more sheltered
and scenic route.

CHAPTER 2

Inside
Passage

Gulf of Alaska

Vancouver
Island

Usual Vancouver to Alaska route

Usual Seattle to Alaska route

CHAPTER 1

Seymour Narrows

North Pacific
Ocean

Victoria

Vancouver

Washington, USA

Seattle

Contents

Ports and Places

When I was a green kid of 18, I had a powerful experience: my first Alaska job - on a fish buying boat working for a native cannery on a remote island. Mickey Hansen, the grizzled Norwegian mate, with fifty seasons "up North" took me under his wing. Taught me the tricks of salmon fishing: how to tell the valuable red salmon from similar looking but much less valuable dog salmon. How to pick our way into an uncharted, rocky harbor.

And more than that: he taught me the lore and legends of The North. It seemed like that kindly old man had a story about each harbor we passed or channel we transited: "We went in there in the old *Mary A,* winter of '31. Thick o' snow, we'd toot that horn and listen for the echo off the rocks, through the snow." In this way he instilled in me a passion for The North that continues to this day.

For me that long ago summer of 1965 was ALASKA in capital letters. There were totems at the dock, eagles in the trees. All I wanted to do afterwards was to go up there to fish commercially in my own boat.

Eventually I did, building a tiny waterfront cabin near a small roadless, fishing settlement.

Our store floated on logs, and was also a bar. The bartender was the fish buyer. You could sell your fish for bar credit and get right to work: whiskey and water, whiskey and coke, or whiskey and Tang. And they saved the ice for the fish.

In the spring we fished the windy outside coast. In the summer, we worked nearby Sumner Strait. In the fall we traveled north to the natural wind tunnel called Lynn Canal, for the 10-dollar-a-fish chum salmon. And in the long, kerosene lantern-lit winters, there was time for visiting.

The stories came out. The experiences of my friends and neighbors, an oral history of the coast. I was an amateur photographer, and a writer. "Write a book," my friends said, "Tell our story." One book became another.

When I first started fishing, cruise ships were few and small. Then more ships began traveling the coast, and I designed a series of illustrated maps to better share with these new visitors the drama and beauty of The North.

For me the books and maps are a way to share with you a sense of the mystery and the power of this place that is such a big part of my life.

So come, take this journey through this land that remains much as it was when the first explorers came through.

Top: Cape Decison lighthouse, mile 775 with Cape Ommaney in the distance, Right: Mickey Hansen and me, Southeast Alaska, 1965. Left: Marchers, Native Festival, Juneau, 2009

Top: Whale watchers in Johnstone Strait, 250 miles north of Vancouver. Below: Star Princess at Juneau.

Headed "Up North?" Taking an Alaska cruise is probably one of the best travel values you'll ever find. Here are some things to consider. First come itineraries; there are several choices:

Seattle to Seattle round trip: Generally the most afford-able cruises, these typically make two or three port calls, plus part of a day at either Glacier Bay, Hubbard Glacier, or Tracy Arm. While these are often billed as 'Inside Passage' cruises, their route usually is up the west or out-side coast of Vancouver Island rather than the scenic tra-ditional Inside Passage through the narrower channels east of Vancouver Island.

Vancouver to Vancouver round trip: Like Seattle sail-ings, these offer usually three ports and glacier viewing. Modestly priced in that you didn't have to fly back from Alaska as you would with a one way cruise, and also offering the advantage of traveling both northbound and southbound up the traditional and very scenic Inside Passage, east of Vancouver Island

Vancouver to Seward or Whittier: One way cruises either to or from Alaska, offering an additional part of a day of glacier viewing, usually at College Fjord in Prince William Sound. A particular advantage of these cruises are that they afford you an opportunity to explore interi-or as well as coastal Alaska. The most popular add-on itin-erary is to spend a day or two in both Fairbanks and Anchorage, take one of the wonderful vistadome style railroad cars on the Alaska Railroad between those towns, combined with a one or two day stopover in the Denali or

McKinley National Park area. Many families will start with a Seattle or Vancouver round trip cruise, and then follow up in later years with a one way cruise combined with a week or so exploring Alaska's great interior.

Other itineraries: San Francisco - Alaska round trip, usually works out to a 10 day cruise, with two sea days on either end, usually includes Victoria and a second day of glacier watching.

Which ship? There's a lot of choice here; presently some 25 large and a dozen or so smaller ships operate on the Alaska run. Today's big Alaska cruise ships are essentially floating resorts with multiple restaurants, extensive shopping, elegant theatres, a wide variety of art, and many public spaces. Free dining (most drinks extra) is usually offered in the large formal dining rooms as well as in a large buffet area on the upper decks. The most recent trend is to charge a fee in the smaller, themed, restaurants, typically $15 - $20 a person, a modest price for the excellent food and service you will usually receive. Take some time to check out the restaurant choices aboard your ship. Some ships, like the *Coral, Sun,* and *Dawn Princess* create a white tablecloth steakhouse in part of the Horizon Court area near the bow. With a stunning view out to the passing landscape, it is a memorable eating experience.

A very valuable feature for ships operating in Alaska is an eating or viewing area that stretches the full width of the front of the ship on an upper deck. You may find eating buffet style with a 180 degree view preferable to the traditional dining rooms, with full service and presentation, but usually little view.

Above: an Alaska cruise is essentially travleling through an ever-changing landscape aboard a floating resort. This is approaching Skagway around 6 in the morning aboard the Sun Princess. Below: getting into the ice is a highlight of any Alaska cruise. This is the Linblad Expeditions Sea Lion

Above: Small ships, like those operated by Alaskan Dream Cruises and Lindblad Expeditions usually have small craft like these Zodiac Inflatibles for exploring, like this group headed out to explore a sea lion rookery.
Below: Shore party on the steep sides of Tracy Arm, near where it divides into two smaller arms.
Right: the Catalyst, seen in Fords Terror, Alaska, takes smaller groups of 8-12 passengers.

Usually carrying 100 passengers or less, small ships offer a very different experience. The focus is much less on entertainment–floor shows, casino gambling, etc.–and more on the history, wildlife, and culture of the passing landscape. Many small ships have daily presentations by one or more naturalists, and have a more flexible schedule allowing them to linger, say when a pod of orcas was sighted, than the larger ships which often have tighter schedules.

The atmosphere on board is apt to be very informal, with perhaps a cocktail hour discussion of the day's activities, and ship's staff often joining passengers for meals.

One of the biggest advantages of small ship cruising is simply that they go where the big ships can't, stopping at off the beaten track towns like Petersburg and Wrangell, or poking into exquisite little coves. In recent years most small ships operating in Alaska carry kayaks and/or Zodiacs, sturdy inflatable boats which are often launched at sites of particular interest like bird rookeries and sea lion haul outs.

Prices are usually significantly higher than for similar accommodations aboard the big cruise ships.

The major companies offering small ship Alaska cruises are Alaskan Dream Cruises, based in Sitka, and Lindblad Expeditions, based in Seattle.

Oops..

When one small chartered vessel anchored inside remote Ford's Terror, the current swung her onto the gravel shore, with the tide dropping. Worried about a possible capsize, the skipper put all the 8 passengers ashore around a campfire for the night. Most stayed awake all night awed at the scenery - it was a rare starry night - and the eyes of the curious animals. In the morning they motored safely away. At the end of the cruise, which featured a dramatic visit to Glacier Bay, the passengers were asked what was their favorite day. All voted for that unscheduled night on the beach of Ford's Terror!

It's only formal if you want it to be. Don't feel like you have to bring suits and dresses unless that is your style. Alaska is a very casual place, and on board your ship there are always other places to eat than the main dining room on formal night.

Bring binoculars. Generally on board ship, anything over 10 power might not be a good choice because of the ship's motion. If you didn't bring any, consider buying them on board. Always bring them when you leave the cabin.

Bring fleece and raingear. Southeast Alaska is a rainy place, but generally the rain is of the light misting variety. So if you have a good rain jacket, you won't be bothered too much. Don't worry about rainpants unless you're determined to hike, rain or not. Make sure you have at least one good warm fleece that you can layer under a jacket. Especially on glacier day, it can get mighty chilly on deck.

Explore your ship early. These big ships have a lot of nifty little places to hang out and watch the passing scene. Don't discover them on the last day.

Eat where there's a view. I can't emphasize this enough, especially on ships that have a forward eating area on an upper deck. You don't have to eat in the formal dining room. Especially on your first night out, you'll be missing some truly spectacular scenery if you don't

Always look for whales. Although most ships have naturalists with a beeper who can be called to the bridge if there is a whale sighting, there are a lot of competing activities on board, and the whales may or may not be announced. Know what to look for: a puff of what looks like smoke, easily seen from a distance. It is a whale exhaling. If you know what to look for, you'll see a lot more whales.

Those Great Ships!

Top: Norwegian Pearl looking south down Gastineau Channel, Juneau. Left: Lounge, Carnival Spirit. Above: Mural aboard the Westerdam. Far left: Looking up at the Mt. Roberts Tramway, from the pool area of the Celebrity Cruise Line Infinity

Alaska shore excursions are a tradition going back to the early 1900s, when passengers from the old steamer *Queen* would be rowed ashore at the foot of Muir Glacier where ladders were set up allowing them to clamber across the top of the glacier, crevasses and all. Imagine what the US Park Service would do if you tried that today!

Today at each port you are offered a wide variety of excursions and more and more cruise lines are encouraging passengers to pre-book by internet before their cruise. If you didn't, then probably you should spend some time with the shore excursions staff or materials and make your choice early in your cruise, as excursions fill up early. If your first and second choices are full, don't despair. On the dock of each cruise port are cruise vendors offering similar excursions to those offered on board. You can generally take these excursions with full confidence. The only wrinkle is that the cruise lines will often say that they won't wait for a passenger on a 'brand x' excursion if he or she is late getting back to the ship. But the truth of the matter is that cruise ships are very reluctant to leave guests behind for any reason.

Generally I recommend that first time Alaska cruisers have at least one flightseeing experience, whether by helicopter or floatplane. If the visibility is good, a Misty Fjords flight from Ketchikan is very dramatic, and the helicopter and land on the glaciers programs offered in Skagway and Juneau are very popular. An expensive but very popular option is the flightseeing/ dogsled excursion where you land on a snowfield and go on a great dogsled ride. The dogs get sooo excited whenever a chopper lands!

The Yukon & White Pass train in Skagway is the most popular shore excursion in the state, and comes in many flavors; at the least I suggest the ride up to the top of the pass and return.

If you haven't seen your quota of whales, the whale watching excursions out of Juneau are excellent, often yielding sightings of both orcas and humpbacks.

Shore

Excursions

The South End

Seattle, Mile Zero to Cape Scott, Mile 280W

"I could not possibly believe that any uncultivated country had ever been discovered exhibiting so rich a picture..."
- Captain George Vancouver, upon first entering Puget Sound, May 1792.

This is stunning country; the drama of the mountains and the sea is everywhere; when the sun comes out suddenly after a long dreary week, the sight of Rainier looming over Seattle and Puget Sound is literally spectacular enough to stop you in your tracks.

These are big, big mountains, 6,000 footers on the west and all the way up to 14,000 foot plus on the east. Their tops are snow covered year round, and the range on the east, the North Cascades, is high enough to scrape much of the water out of the clouds as they head east. So much so that Eastern Washington seems like a different state–dry, the summers much hotter, the winters much colder.

The ring of fire is very present here–some of the earth's great plates that form the crust meet along the ridge of the North Cascades. If you fly in or out, look as your plane gets up over the mountains and if it's clear you'll see a chain of volcanoes: Rainier, Adams, St. Helens, and Hood, stretching out of sight to the south.

Volcanoes are still active; after two months of throat clearing, Mt. St. Helens blew the top 1,300 feet of mountain and a cubic mile of ash into the atmosphere in May of 1980.

Much of the east side of the Sound, the Seattle - Tacoma - Everett corridor is fast paced, growing rapidly with all the attendant problems: congestion, traffic, pollution and noise.

Across the sound is very different. The old Puget Sound of cedar bungalows, forests sloping to the water's edge, driftwood fires, soaring eagles, and native settlements lingers here.

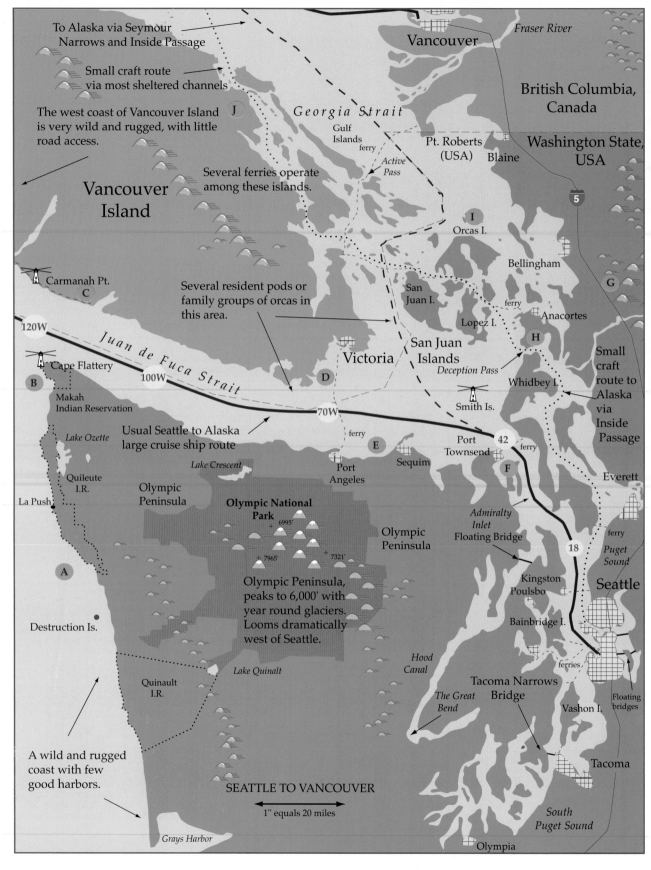

To Alaska via Seymour
Narrows and Inside Passage

Small craft route
via most sheltered channels

The west coast of Vancouver Island
is very wild and rugged, with little
road access.

Fraser River

Vancouver

British Columbia,
Canada

Georgia Strait

Gulf
Islands
ferry

Pt. Roberts
(USA) Blaine

Washington State,
USA

J

*Active
Pass*

Vancouver
Island

Several ferries operate
among these islands.

I

Orcas I.

Bellingham

G

Carmanah Pt.

C

Several resident pods or
family groups of orcas in
this area.

San
Juan I.

Lopez I.

Anacortes

H

ferry

120W

Juan de Fuca Strait

Cape Flattery

100W

Victoria

San Juan
Islands

Deception Pass

Small
craft
route
to
Alaska
via
Inside
Passage

B

Makah
Indian Reservation

D

70W

Smith Is.

Whidbey I.

Usual Seattle to Alaska
large cruise ship route

Lake Ozette

Quileute
I.R.

La Push

A

Olympic
Peninsula

Lake Crescent

ferry

Port
Angeles

E

Sequim

Port
Townsend

42

ferry

F

Everett

ferry

**Olympic National
Park**

+ 6995'

Olympic
Peninsula

*Admiralty
Inlet*
Floating Bridge

18

*Puget
Sound*

Seattle

Destruction Is.

+ 7965' + 7321'

Olympic Peninsula,
peaks to 6,000' with
year round glaciers.
Looms dramatically
west of Seattle.

*Hood
Canal*

Kingston
Poulsbo

Bainbridge I.

ferries

Floating
bridges

Quinault
I.R.

Lake Quinalt

*The Great
Bend*

**Tacoma Narrows
Bridge**

Vashon I.

A wild and rugged
coast with few
good harbors.

SEATTLE TO VANCOUVER

1" equals 20 miles

Tacoma

Grays Harbor

*South
Puget
Sound*

Olympia

A - The outside coast of Washington State is easily the most rugged shore of the lower 48 states. There is little road access, and much of the shore is Indian reservations. In most places along the northwest section, the only way to get down to the actual shore is via several miles of very rugged trail, but the walk is worth it. At the end are spectacular beaches with offshore rocks, arches, and spires, and hemmed in on either end by high and dramatic headlands.

B - In recent years the Makah tribe has sought and received permission to conduct a tribal harvest of gray whales, spurring protests by several whale conservation and environmental groups.

C - The West Coast Trail was originally built as an aid to shipwrecked mariners. Today it's a challenging hiking trail with crude suspension bridges, and vertical ladders in and out of ravines. Not for novices! 4-7 days, no services, and no way out except at either end.

D - Pedder Bay. In the 1970s and 80s orcas used to congregate here and hunters, seeking to capture them for sale to public aquariums. set their nets here around Orca schools. Orca capture was banned in British Columbia in 1986.

E - Rain shadow effect. In the Pacific Northwest, weather generally comes from the southwest, off the ocean. However, the mountains of the Olympic Peninsula are high enough to scrape the rain out of the passing clouds. This rain shadow creates a micro climate in the Sequim area which is much sunnier and drier than in Seattle.

F - Entrance to Puget Sound. Strong tide rips here and heavy seas when wind and tide are opposed to each other. The big cross sound ferry here frequently cancels trips when the seas build too high. Before World War II three forts here guarded the entrance with big bore cannons.

G - North Cascade Mountain Range. A forty mile wide band of extremely rugged mountains, whose foothills extends west to the edge of the urban Tacoma - Everett corridor. Only three year-round roads cross this range, which are frequently closed in winter with heavy snows and avalanches. These mountains scrape most of the moisture out of the eastward flowing clouds, creating the much, much drier and hotter (colder in the winter) climate of eastern Washington.

H - Deception Pass–narrow, steep sided, tide wracked, with a high bridge over it, Northwest boaters have learned to read their tide tables carefully here.

I - Matia Island, one of Washington state's exquisite marine parks, some of which are for the exclusive use of boaters in kayaks or other non motorized craft.

J - Small craft route north winds through the most sheltered channels.

Top: Cruise ship Oosterdam passing Point Wilson, Mile 42, the transition between sheltered and more open waters. Bottom: 14,000 Mount Rainier looms over the Seattle skyline.

SEATTLE
The Emerald City

Each morning tens of thousands of commuters cross the generally calm waters of Puget Sound from sleepy bedroom communities 'across the water' to their work places along the busy Tacoma-Everett corridor. Particularly for those who walk on, it can be a very pleasant arrangement. The ferry takes you right to downtown Seattle, where, if you are lucky, work is just a brisk walk away. For those who must drive on, the commute is a bit more tedious as you might have to get in line an hour or more before sailing. With wireless internet, food, and espresso service, commuting by ferry is becoming an excellent way to get to work without the hassle of freeway travel. Above: Seattle skyline with North Cascade range beyond. Right: Inside the Seattle Art Museum, on 1st avenue, just a couple of blocks up from the ferry dock.

When travelers took the train between New York and Boston and walked on cobblestone streets, the entire Pacific Northwest was thickly forested from mountain to shore, and the only settlements were natives, living easily on the products of forest and sea.

Seattle's first settlers trudged ashore in the pouring rain in November of 1851. The families had braved the rigors of the Oregon Trail, and a stormy trip up the coast by boat. "And for this?" they might have said, as they found out what they had traveled all that way for: a half finished cabin on the edge of the gloomy forest with scowling, half clad natives as a welcoming committee.

Less than a month

later a small schooner dropped anchor in front of the settlers and offered them $1000 for a load of fir pilings from the forest behind the settlement, and the industry that was to drive the region far into the 20th century, logging and sawmilling, was born.

A century later, the Boeing Aircraft Company was the biggest game in town as it prepared to usher in the jet age with the plane management bet the future of the company on: the 707.

Twenty five years after that, a new industry that would truly transform the region and the world was beginning just east of Seattle: computer software and the amazing rise of Microsoft.

Today Seattle has a broad based economy where Boeing and Microsoft are still the employment leaders, and a very outdoor oriented population. A climate that allows either skiing or sailing on almost any day from Thanksgiving to Easter and a dress code where bluejeans and a clean shirt will get you in almost anywhere, has made Seattle and the Northwest very popular with young professionals.

Does it really rain all the time? Actually New York (43" annually) and Kansas City (50") are a both a lot wetter than Seattle's average 38 inches. It's just that Seattle's is often spread out over more days.

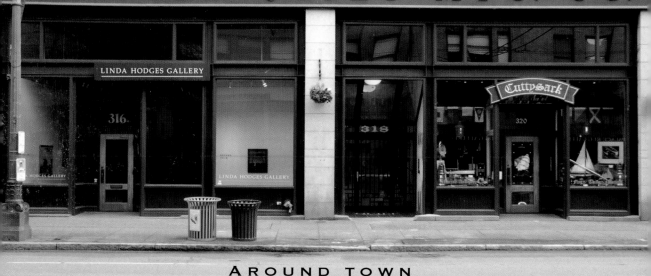

Pioneer Square:
This area of First Avenue, at the southern end of downtown is an eclectic collection of galleries, shops, ethnic restaurants, the excellent Gold Rush Museum, and lots of street art. Additionally the highly recommended Seattle Underground Tour begins just off the square. When this part of Seattle was regraded to allow for better movement of streetcars and sewage, the streets were lifted a whole floor. The old building fronts are still there, in sort of this weird nether world.

A few well regarded restaurants: Ivar's Acres of Clams, on the waterfront, McCormick and Schmick's, 1103 First Ave; Anthony's Pier 66, waterfront; and Dragonfish Asian Cafe at 722 Pine St.

Pike Place Market is probably the most varied food and craft market on the west coast. Also there are some great places to eat here, overlooking the sound. Exciting!

Seattle Art Museum, on First Avenue, downtown, just finished up a major renovation. Many permanent and rotating collections. Highly recommended.

Fishermen's Terminal & Ballard Locks – Much of the Alaska fishing fleet, including some of the king crab boats from The Deadliest Catch are based here.

Waterfront & Aquarium – Seattle's waterfront is a hopping place, Right below downtown, it is a collection of shops, restaurants, and excursion vessel docks. The Blake Island tour with salmon dinner and Native American dancing is highly recommended. The IMAX feature on Mt. St. Helens at the Aquarium is excellent.

Museum of Flight, between downtown and the airport, has a recent addition with stunning WWI and II dioramas.

Experience Music Museum in the Seattle Center, downtown. Wonderful historical exhibits and hands on activities, with excellent section on Seattle's own wild and groovy Jimmy Hendrix.

Olympic Sculpture Garden at the north end of the downtown waterfront is a 3 acre spread with graceful sculptures overlooking the water. Opened 2007.

STEHEKIN: BACK IN TIME

Tucked up at the very head of Lake Chelan, accessible only by boat, floatplane and for the very hardy hiker, foot, Stehekin is a bit like stepping into the past. Trails wind past remote homesteads, the oldest apple orchard in the National Forest System, and a few hotels.

About a 3 hour drive from Seattle via either Stevens or Snoqualmie/Blewitt Passes, takes you to the town of Chelan on the sounth of the lake. From there you take The Lady of The Lake II - departure 8:30 a.m. - four hours to Stehekin, with several stops where hikers with big packs might get off to disappear down winding trails back into the hills. The ferry does make a 90 minute stop at Stehekin, but you really should spend a night or town to fully appreciate what's there. A good choice is the **Stehekin Landing Resort** at the dock; see Stehekin.com for others. Bikes and horses are available for rent. A great day hike is just up the winding dirt road to High Bridge, passing the old one room school, a waterfall, and on to High Bridge. From there you can hike for an hour or so up the **Agnes Creek Trail** and make it back to High Bridge to catch the 3 or 6:15 pm shuttle back down the valley. Or if you want to walk downhill, and bus up, the morning shuttle up the valley leaves the boat landing at 8 and 11:15.

GREAT SHORT TRIPS

Olympic Peninsula Loop

Bainbridge ferry to Kitsap Peninsula, to Hood Canal Bridge to Port Angeles, to Forks, and La Push. Return same way or via Queets and Olympia. Alternate stop at Hurricane Ridge S. of Port Angeles. 1-? days

North Cascades Loop

I-5 north to Burlington, east on North Cascades Highway to Okanogan, follow Columbia River S. to Wenatchee, then Rt. 2 over Stevens Pass back to I-5. Don't miss Winthrop and Levenworth. 2 days.

Victoria Clipper

Day trip from Seattle waterfront to downtown Victoria, truly an exquisite destination.

Vancouver by Train

This is a wonderful day trip–Amtrak, leaves around 7:45, cruises along the shore of Puget Sound and up through gorgeous farm country, arrives 11:30. Explore Vancouver and return on the 6 pm dinner train!

Mt. St. Helens

Day trip to Mt. St. Helens National Monument–four hours each way, but dramatic vistas and good visitor center.

Top: Wooden skiff aboard schooner Adventure at Port Townsend. Just two hours from Seattle by ferry and car, this Victorian seaside town is a center for woodenboat craftsmen. Below: Second Beach, near La Push, WA.

Top: Square rigger with about a 12 foot high deck load of gorgeous Douglas Fir planks and beams from a Puget Sound mill. Opposite page: Port Blakely, Bainbridge Island around 1880. The uncropped image shows seven full rigged ships and seven big schooners, all loading lumber from the big mill at Port Blakely. remains. SFM F12.21.725m Below: Loading lumber from the old sawmill, Mendocino, CA, around 1890. And if the weather came up, the ship had to leave. Consider how much easier it was to load in a place like Port Blakely on right. SFMM

When the timber barons came to Puget Sound, it was not just the trees that awed them. They were used to big Dougas Firs on the California and Oregon coasts, but it was the harbors! On those bold coasts the ships could only get in to load lumber in the best of conditions because there were hardly any harbors worthy of the word.

In places there was wonderful timber but no harbors at all. Ships had to run a cable from their mast to the dock while they lay at an exposed mooring, like in the photo on the left, and tediously receive lumber by cable, steam up in their boilers, ready to leave immediately if the weather deteriorated.

But in Puget Sound it was the combination of good harbors and protected waters next to great stands of trees that created the vast timber economy that was to dominate the region for its first hundred years. Port Blakely, Port Madison, Port Gamble, Port Ludlow, and other sheltered sleepy coves became the destination of ships from all over the world as big mills and little towns sprang up to harvest the great trees and load them aboard ships. Recently timber frame builders have been salvaging the Doug Fir out of old warehouses, mines, and mills and recycling them into new homes and offices.

THE MIGHTY EMPIRE
OF THE WOODS

Top: Sailor on a summer evening in Port Madison, Bainbridge Island. Just 15 minutes from the ferry to downtown Seattle, Port Madison is one of Puget Sound's many exquisite harbors. Once site of a large sawmill, today it is an elegant waterfront community.. Bottom: Morning commuter ferry pulling into the dock at Kingston, 15 miles northwest of downtown Seattle, with Mt. Rainier in the background. Not a bad view for your morning commute!

Over time the great stands of timber around the sawmill towns were cut, and many mills closed or relocated to less valuable land where logs cut in more distant forests could be brought by tug and barge.

As the logging and mill jobs disappeared, workers from across the sound discovered the pleasures of having summer homes in the waterfront communities on the west side of the Sound. A 'Mosquito Fleet' of small steamboats sprang up to move people and freight back and forth. Then as Seattle grew, more and more families discovered the benefits of living 'across the water,' with the primary worker commuting on the fleet of larger and faster ferries.

Seattle's growth really took off in the 1990s, and the traffic across the two Lake Washington bridges and along the region's freeways became more and more intense, furthering the interest in homes across Puget Sound. Today families here have to travel further and further to find housing they can afford. It is not uncommon for people to travel 45 minutes or more to the ferry dock to wait to get on the ferry for the 35 minute or hour plus ride to downtown Seattle, depending on the run.

Seattle itineraries depart from the waterfront, site of all the action in the 1897-98 Yukon gold rush, when it was crowded with men seeking passage north to make their fortune and merchants trying to make their fortune selling supplies...

Have a look at the steeply sloped waterfront north of

the city. In really wet winters, these hillsides get super saturated and the homes occasionally slide to the bottom.

A few miles north of the Edmonds Ferry Terminal on the east at **mile 19**, Port Susan and Everett harbor open to the right or east of your ship. Over the bluff here is The Boeing Aircraft Companies big plant, home to the amazingly venerable 747, 777, and now the new "Dreamliner," the fuel efficient 787.

Small craft headed to Alaska like to stay in the narrowest waters and unless the tides and the weather forecast are both perfect, usually branch off here, taking a scenic, but more winding route up to the San Juan Islands and then on into Canada. A favorite stop for these boats is **La Conner**, a very picturesque small town located along the shores of the Swinomish Slough. This area is all very fertile bottomland, part of the Skagit River delta. Hundreds of acres are planted in flowers, and a popular event each spring is the Tulip Festival.

At **mile 39**, the Point Wilson Lighthouse, your ship and the landscape make a major change. Just south of here is the **Deadly Triangle**, where the cannons from three forts once created an overlapping field of fire, through which no enemy ship could pass unscathed.

Point Wilson is the intersection between the sheltered waters of Puget Sound and the much wider and windier waters of the Strait of Juan de Fuca. It was somewhere around here that Captain George Vancouver, the English Navy Captain who first explored and charted much of the northwest coast made his famous observation on page 19 which history proved correct.

The Boeing Aircraft Company, circa 1915, when lightweight Sitka spruce was a major structural component. It's a lot different now. MOHAI 9274A Bottom: Schooner Adventure passes downtown Port Townsend.

You'll probably be busy, exploring the ship, unpacking, meeting up with friends, etc. but the Point Wilson area, beginning around mile 37, is a major transition, so you should be ready to have a look around. Typically, once your ship gets moving at full speed, it will be traveling around twenty miles an hour, so figure less than two hours to get up to the Point Wilson area. after you leave Seattle.

Above: Sleepy Coupeville, on Whidbey Island. Small craft bound to Alaska or the San Juan Islands often take a route to the east of Whidbey.

Mile 40: Point Wilson lighthouse marks the transition from sheltered to more open waters.

There is a lot of tidal current here; look for tide tips close to the point, as well as sea lions and seals having a nice supper on the salmon which are swept by the tide close to the point.

The landscape changes dramatically at Point Wilson. Narrow Puget Sound opens up to the wide Strait of Juan de Fuca. Most large cruise ships leaving Seattle for Alaska will turn to the west here, staying to the right or north side of the traffic lanes as they parallel the Washington coast, along the US-Canada border.

On the bluff to the west at **Mile 38** is **Port Townsend,** a decidedly Victorian town with a wonderfully eclectic flavor. Realtors had really gotten excited in the 1880s when for a time it looked as if The Northern Pacific Railroad would select PT (as it is known locally) as its western terminal, but after a geography check, the NPRR wisely chose Tacoma instead. So while Seattle and Tacoma boomed, Port Townsend grew at a much slower pace, with Victorian style houses perched on the steep hills around town with commanding views of the intersection of Puget Sound and Juan de Fuca Strait.

If you look closely, just north of town, and south of the lighthouse at Point Wilson, you'll see what looks a bit like a New England college campus. This is Fort Worden, one of three major US Army facilities situated on the three points overlooking the entrance to Puget Sound. The fields of fire from their hidden cannons formed a killing zone to prevent enemy ships from entering Puget Sound. Today the cannons are gone, but the forts are available for rent and are busy with many functions year round from soccer tournaments to sea kayaking symposiums.

Six hours north of Seattle, you'll enter a very different world.

About six hours after your ship leaves Seattle, you'll be at the place that sailors truly dreaded before the advent of electronic aids to navigation. For decades, "Lost off Cape Flattery without a trace" was the epitaph for too many ships. This was the entrance to the Strait of Juan de Fuca, an area of strong currents and frequent fogs. Captain Cook, exploring the coast, never found this ten mile wide entrance, wisely staying out of the fog near the coast.

The consequences of a navigational error were severe; the coasts of northwest Washington and Vancouver Island were fringed with reefs, isolated spires, and rocks. The surf was almost always heavy and any ship caught in its grip would be quickly destroyed.

Tugboat skippers knew how sailing masters felt about the entrance to the strait, and in those days before good radio communications, would patrol the entrance, hoping to pick up a big square rigger, anxious about the weather and looking for a tow up the strait to its final destination.

So many ships were lost along the British Columbia shore north of Cape Flattery that a trail was constructed along the very rugged shore of Vancouver Island, north of the entrance to the Strait. At intervals cabins were built, stocked with food, firewood, and a telephone to the nearest lighthouse.

The overnight passage from Seattle takes you to a very different land. Gone are the waterfront homes, a road that follows the shore, lights at night, buildings or other signs of man seen by day.

Top: Norwegian Star, nearing the west end of the Strait of Juan de Fuca, an area that used to be mightily feared by sailors. Below: brass octopus sculpture on a Port Townsend boat.. The town is a major crafts and wooden boat center.

"A place in the San Juans" was the ultimate for north-westerners–a little waterfront bungalow somewhere among the large and small islands of this sleepy archipelago, just 50 miles north of Seattle. With four major islands served by ferries out of Anacortes, and dozens of smaller ones, they are a major destination for vacationers. In recent years the price for all land has shot up, and a bit of a two tier society has developed with teachers and other workers finding it very hard to find affordable places to buy. It is also a place where the pace of life in the winter slows way down, especially on the smaller islands. There are a number of summer camps here where generations of Northwest families have sent their children. These photos are Camp Four Winds, on Orcas Island.

THE SAN JUAN ISLANDS

The west coast of Vancouver island is very rugged, open to the full force of the storms that drive in off the North Pacific. It is also almost completely isolated from the busy east coast. Only a couple of roads penetrate the difficult interior of the island, essentially upgraded logging roads, winding and potholed.

For most of the 20th century, the economy here was almost totally resource driven-salmon, herring, halibut, and timber. You were either producing them, processing them, or supporting the folks who did.

If someone had told a West Coast logger or fishermen in the boom years of the 1950s that a new economy would come to the coast, based on whale watching, kayaking, eco tours, and vacationers, chances are he might have fallen over backwards laughing in disbelief. Back then the life was so rough, so rugged, so remote from anything not connected immediately to the business at hand–logging and fishing–that a change of that dimension seemed totally out of the question.

Yet this is exactly what happened. The salmon stocks that the West Coast fishermen depended on slumped badly in the 1970s and 1980s, due to a combination of mismanagement–overfishing–and damage done to salmon habitat. At the same time a growing awareness by the native tribes and commercial fishermen of the ecological damage of certain logging practices led to logging restrictions.

Fortunately the new economy, based on eco tourism, surfers, kayakers, whale watchers, fish farming and Vancouverites looking for second homes came along just when the old was disappearing

Top: few places on the North American coast are as remote and rugged as Vancouver Island's West Coast. Below: wet suits needed; you may have to hike through the woods to get to some of the good beaches.

> ── Passenger Tip ──
> There's a lot to do aboard ship your first night out, but this landscape is really worth seeing. Find a place in the front part of your ship with a good view forward and just sit for a bit and look at the changing scene.

VICTORIA

Below: houseboat along the water-front path between the cruise docks and downtown - a fun 30 minute walk - there is also a shuttle.
 Most ships only stop in the evening, so taking the shuttle ($7.50, cash only) at least one way saves time.

While Vancouver—just 75 miles to the NW—is a totally cosmopolitan modern city with a heavy sprinkling of Asian immigrants, Victoria seems a bit more like a taste of Olde England. The British fondness for gardens is especially evident in the many private and public gardens and plantings that line its streets.

Originally settled when a Hudson's Bay Company trading post was established here in 1843, this city and Vancouver Island became a crown colony in 1849. Ten years later another colony was established on the mainland to support the many prospectors that had arrived with the 1858 Fraser River gold strike. Eventually the two colonies merged to form what is today British Columbia and Victoria became its administrative capital, while Vancouver became the industrial center.

Victoria is a good place to shop for First Nations (coastal native) art and craft souvenirs. Additionally many shops specialize in goods from England that would be hard to find elsewhere on your cruise.

What to see: Fortunately, many of Victoria's attractions are centered around the harbor:

The Royal British Columbia Museum is one of the best small museums you'll ever encounter. If you want to see Northwest Native culture up close, this will be probably your best opportunity. While the tribes in British Columbia are distinct from those along the areas of Coastal Alaska that you will be traveling through, their art such as totem poles share many of the same themes.

Top: the Victoria Clipper provides hydrofoil service downtown to downtown between Seattle and Victoria. Below: Inside the Bengal Lounge at the Empress Hotel. Left: orca statue and the Empress dominate the waterfront.

Top: dessert tray at afternoon tea at The Empress Hotel. Bottom: sign on truck - actually Victoria is a great place to get out and go whale watching - there is a resident pod of orcas usually nearby and there are fast boats that leave from the harbor downtown.

The Empress Hotel was part of a series of large and very notable resorts built by the Canadian Pacific Railway. Make a point of visiting the restored lobby, where afternoon tea is a major local event.

Across the harbor are the seaplane docks and the booking and boarding area for **whale watching tours.** This area is particularly suited for seeing orcas or killer whales.

12 miles from downtown are **Butchart Gardens**, which has become one of the most visited sites in the province. What is now a stunning 50 acre showpiece had rather humble beginnings. In 1904 Jennnie Butchart, whose husband operated a cement plant near the site, got tired of staring at the ugly scar in the land that his limestone quarrying operations left. She brought in a few plants to spruce up the area and one thing led to another!

IN BUTCHART GARDENS

EXCURSIONS

Butchart Gardens
English Tea at Butchart Gardens
Victoria Pub Tour
Craigdarroch Castle, Mt. Tolmie
    & City Highlights
Double-Decker City Highlights
Victoria by Horse-Drawn Trolley
Whale Watching Cruise
Shuttle to downtown
NOTE: Excursions may change;
    check on board.

VANCOUVER

Like most Northwest coast cities, forest products played a huge part in Vancouver's history, with big square riggers waiting to take lumber to Asian, Australian, and Pacific ports as soon as it could be milled. It still continues today. When you cross the Fraser River entering the city, look down and most likely you'll see BC's premier product, logs, (some say marijuana is the province's biggest export...) traveling by barge or raft to a sawmill or a waiting ship.

With one of the best harbors on the coast and good road and rail connections, it quickly developed into Canada's premier west coast port as well. With a dramatic mountain and waterfront setting, the city became one of the favorite spots in the British Empire within a few decades of being founded, as evidenced by the many large and elegant Victorian era homes.

In more modern times, concerns about what would happen in Hong Kong after the mainland Chinese took over in 1997 led to the arrival of large numbers of Chinese immigrants, many of whom brought substantial personal wealth with them. The result is a noticeably multi-ethnic city with the second biggest Chinatown in North America.

Around town: Many of the sights are easily accessible from where your ship docks. Within walking or short taxi distance is much of the city core with almost unlimited shopping and dining. There is also a subway/elevated rail system called the Skytrain which makes getting around fairly simple.

A few blocks east of Canada Place is **Gastown**, where the city was first settled, and today is an eclectic neighborhood

Opposite: Granville Island, close to downtown is a delightful place with many places to eat and a huge market. Top: Restored salmon boat at Granville Island. Bottom: Aquabusses connect places along the Vancouver waterfront.

41

Above: Dawn Princess heads out under the Lion's Gate Bridge on her way to Alaska. Below: Part of the excellent totem display at Vancouver's Stanley Park, a 20 minute walk from Canada Place.

of old warehouses made into restaurants, artist's lofts, condos, and all manner of shops.

Chinatown is a few more blocks to the south (consider a taxi) and its size reflects Vancouver's popularity with Asians. This is the real thing! If you don't read Chinese, make sure your menu has English as well. With the waters of Georgia Strait and the North Pacific close at hand, many restaurants feature live tanks from which patrons may select their meal.

Visitors and Vancouverites alike are indeed fortunate that its founders set aside the 1,000 or so acres that today is **Stanley Park**. It features restaurants, a zoo, the ubiquitous totems, but most of all a stunning waterfront setting right next to downtown. A popular walk leads through the park to a dramatic overlook at Lion's Gate.

Take the foot ferry to **Granville Island** on False Creek. Granville Island is a combination of a farmer's and craftsmen's market, with restaurants. These foot ferries or **Aquabusses,** are also just a good inexpensive way to see town from the water!

Within walking distance west of Granville Island is the **Vancouver Maritime Museum**, whose showpiece exhibit is the brave little steamer *St. Roche*, which much of her epic two year Vancouver to Newfoundland transit frozen into the Arctic ice.

Fly to Victoria - floatplanes operate almost hourly from the docks right next to Canada Place, where many ships leave from. The 30 minute flight gives you a spectacular view of the Gulf Islands and lands right in downtown Victoria. **Explore the Gulf Islands** by ferry and car. Take a few days; there are many islands and ferries: Saltspring Island is my favorite.

EXCURSIONS

Stanley Park Visit and City Highlights
City Sights & Capillano Canyon Walk
Scenic Trolley Around City, China-
town and Vancouver lookout
NOTE: Excursions may change;
check on board.

Top left: aquabus and condos. Top right: Chinatown street sign. Bottom left: steam powered clock in Gastown - whistles on the
hour and half hour. Bottom right: Eskimo art
in downtown shop.

43

CHAPTER 2

The Wilderness Begins

Vancouver, B.C., Mile 95,

to Alaska Border, Mile 575W

"Tracing shining ways through fiord and sound, past forests and waterfalls, islands and mountains and far azure headlands, it seems as if surely we must at length reach the very paradise of the poets, the abode of the blessed."

- John Muir, *Travels in Alaska*

Top: Kayaker in Johnstone Strait, around mile 242. North Coast. Pacific Rim Paddling photo. Below: Turn Pt Lighthouse, on the US - Canada border, with bulk carrier headed for Vancouver.

Look to the right a few miles after you pass under Lion's Gate Bridge, leaving Vancouver, to the Point Atkinson Lighthouse. If you want to get a clear sense of what much of the coast of British Columbia and Alaska is like, look beyond the lighthouse.

This is Howe Sound, the first of the many deep and winding inlets that penetrate far into the interior. For example, there is no road around the head of the inlet because the land is too rough; you have to take a ferry across instead.

And it was here that the first explorers, like British Captain George Vancouver, who explored and named

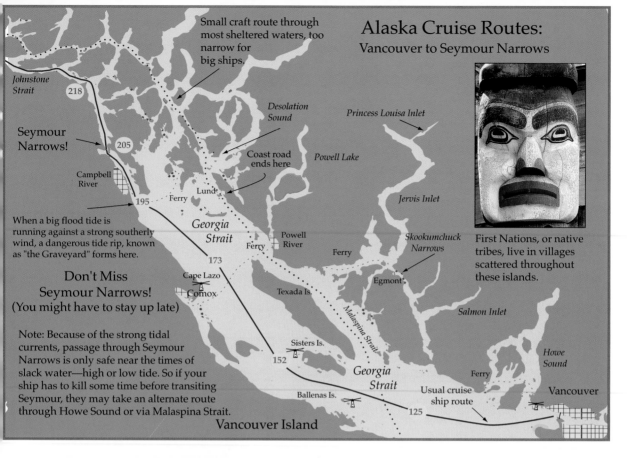

Alaska Cruise Routes:
Vancouver to Seymour Narrows

Small craft route through most sheltered waters, too narrow for big ships.

Johnstone Strait 218

Desolation Sound

Princess Louisa Inlet

Powell Lake

Seymour Narrows! 205

Coast road ends here

Georgia Strait

Jervis Inlet

Campbell River

Lund   *Ferry*

195   *Ferry*

When a big flood tide is running against a strong southerly wind, a dangerous tide rip, known as "the Graveyard" forms here.

Skookumchuck Narrows

173   Powell River   *Ferry*

Ferry

Don't Miss Seymour Narrows!
(You might have to stay up late)

Cape Lazo
Comox

Texada Is.

Egmont

First Nations, or native tribes, live in villages scattered throughout these islands.

Note: Because of the strong tidal currents, passage through Seymour Narrows is only safe near the times of slack water—high or low tide. So if your ship has to kill some time before transiting Seymour, they may take an alternate route through Howe Sound or via Malaspina Strait.

Malaspina Strait

Salmon Inlet

Sisters Is.

152   *Georgia Strait*

Ballenas Is.   Usual cruise ship route   *Ferry*

Howe Sound

Vancouver

125

Vancouver Island

This is orca territory so keep your eyes peeled - sculpture is next to the pool on the Star Princess.

much of the B.C. and Southeast Alaska coasts, had their first troubles. At the time, the British were under the impression that there was a passage somewhere across or through North America from the Pacific to the Atlantic—the "Northwest Passage"—and his job was to see if it existed. This meant that each promising inlet or channel had to be explored to make sure it wasn't the legendary channel.

Leaving Vancouver, you enter Georgia Strait, sort of an inland sea that is the home to much of the population and industry of lower British Columbia.

It also has a climate that is often noticeably drier from that just a hundred or so miles to the north - the rain shadow effect of the mountains of Vancouver Island. The coast to the east here is nicknamed The Sunshine Coast.

Looking for a great place to retire? The **Gulf Islands**, directly across Georgia Straits, with dozens of islands large and small, served by several ferries, would truly be a great choice. They are particularly popular with boaters, and noticeably less crowded than the **American San Juan Islands**, just across the border to the south. Many Canadians have second homes here, a short ferry ride away from Victoria or Vancouver.

Imagine this: several cubic miles of water must pass through the maze of narrow channels north of Vancouver every six hours. This is the tide pouring in and out of Georgia Strait to the North Pacific.

Unless you are from the Northwest or from Nova Scotia, the tides here are larger than any you probably have encountered before and can have major effects upon mariners traveling here, even on a ship as big as a large cruise ship.

The main effect is in the narrow channels where the tide can create currents up to almost 20 MPH, as well as whirlpools big enough to capsize 60 foot boats! The prudent mariner transits such areas at slack water—near the time of high and low tide.

Once, when I was an incautious young skipper in a 60 footer, I was towing a disabled 36' fishing boat down from Alaska to Seattle. Eager to get home, but too late for safe slack water, I though I could still get through constricted Dodd Narrows against the current. So I went up onto the flying bridge and shouldered our way into the current.

Instantly I knew it was a bad mistake! The current shoved us violently back and forth and I was desperately afraid that the boat I was towing would hit the shore in one of our wild swings. Finally we

Top: Kayaker flips at Skookumchuck Rapids—the effect of the tide here is to create a standing wave, which a skilled kayaker can 'surf' for minutes on end. Above: Oops - this small cruise ship entered Yuculta Rapids while the tide was still running - see current swirls - and rolled far enough for bar bottles and glasses to slide off and break!

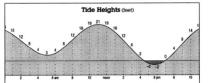

Typical pattern of Northwest tides

got through, and I radioed back to the fellow I was towing, a cool customer, on his 25th season as an Alaska commercial fishermen.

"It wasn't too bad," he answered me, " I had to steer a bit to keep off the rocks. And... I bit my cigar in half..."

EXPLORING THE BC COAST BY FERRY

The BC Ferry system offers a very modest priced way to explore here, island hopping by day, and spending the night in bed and breakfasts, camping, etc. One possibility is to take the ferry across Howe Sound from the Horseshoe Bay terminal north of Vancouver, exploring the Sunshine Coast, ferry across Jervis Inlet to the Powell River area, explore, then ferry across to Vancouver Is.

From there you have even more ferry and island choices.

Explore at www.bcferries.com

Self-loading log barge near Campbell River. Some of these rigs even carry small pusher tugs to move logs around to make loading easier.

Things to look for:

- Log and chip barges: British Columbia is a legendary producer of forest products. Wood chips are moved in big high-sided barges so full they seem almost submerged.
- Log booms: The rectangular rafts of logs towed slowly behind tugs are hard to see at night, because frequently they are marked only by dim and flickering kerosene lamps.
- Alaska-bound tugs and barges from Puget Sound, stacked high with container vans with large items, such as boats, strapped on top.
- The big mills: Most noticeable is Powell River, east of Mile 173, one of the largest in the world.

The REAL Inside Passage: Fraser Reach from 30,000 feet!

To the mariner, "inside" basically means protected, away from the ocean waves and swells, and the effect of a strong wind. And when the Pleistocene glaciers carved out the canyons and fjords of the Northwest about a million years ago, they created the Inside Passage and a boaters paradise.

If there was no Inside Passage and if the coast of British Columbia and Alaska were like that of Oregon and California—bold with great beaches but few harbors—there probably wouldn't be any Alaska cruises either, for there would be no glacial fjords to cruise into or harbors to visit.

The very history of Alaska and British Columbia would have been much different. It was the existence of all these sheltered passageways that allowed travelers, even in the smallest craft to travel north in safety.

When cruise ships were small, say less than 500', they followed the traditional Inside Passage north of Vancouver Island: Milbanke Sound, Lama Passage, Tolmie Channel, Graham and Fraser Reaches, and dramatic quarter mile wide Grenville Channel to Alaska.

Unfortunately for you, almost all of today's very large ships find the traditional route a little too narrow. There are alternate, wider, and still scenic routes, via Caamano Sound and Principe Channel. For some reason, probably a very minor cost savings, you don't need a Canadian pilot. Now most large ships just go straight up Hecate Strait from Vancouver Island to the Alaska border. It might be cheaper, but it sure isn't as scenic.

Above: Particularly for smaller vessels—say under 200'—the myriad winding channels of the Inside Passage offer a better route to Alaska. It's really a shame that Alaska cruise ships have gotten so big that they can't transit these really narrow channels. Right: Small craft take the narrowest channels like the one on the right, but must wait for slack water in the really narrow spots.

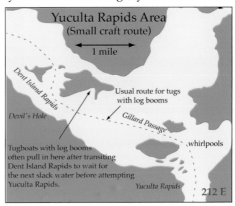

Yuculta Rapids Area
(Small craft route)

1 mile

Dent Island Rapids

Devil's Hole

Usual route for tugs with log booms

Gillard Passage

whirlpools

Tugboats with log booms often pull in here after transiting Dent Island Rapids to wait for the next slack water before attempting Yuculta Rapids.

Yuculta Rapids

212 E

BRITISH COLUMBIA'S SPECIAL PLACES:
GULF ISLANDS

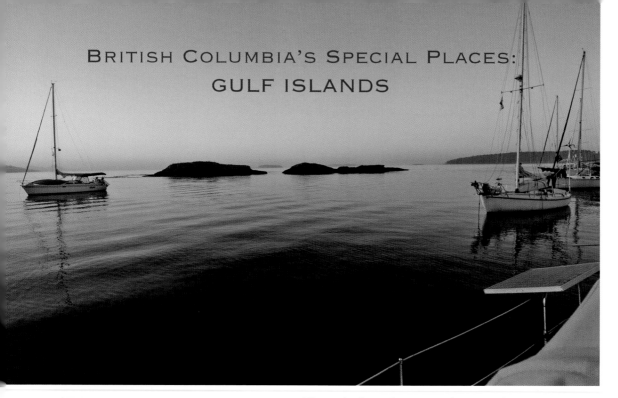

If you look to the west when you leave Vancouver, you'll see a mini - archipelago of islands scattered along the west side of Georgia Strait. Made up of eight larger and numerous smaller islands, they offer a remarkably more laid back lifestyle for their residents than nearby Vancouver or Victoria. And as Pacific weather systems move from the Southwest, losing their moisture over the high mountains of the US Olympic Peninsula, a much drier and sunnier climate is created than most of Puget Sound and upper Vancouver Island.

Top: Sailboats at dawn, at Princess Island, a marine park. Above: braided garlic at the Saltspring Island Saturday market. Right: A hiker enjoys a quiet moment at Tumbo Island.

DESOLATION SOUND

Vancouver Departures: look to the north, or to the right of your ship's course with the last of the daylight. If it is at all clear, you should be able to see the dramatic mountains in the Desolation Sound area, west of about **mile 180** on your map.

This is easily the most misnamed place on the entire coast: it is totally spectacular and almost all a protected marine park. Plus the salt water is warm enough for great swimming and oysters grow wild on the shores! For boaters it doesn't get much better than that. We were here in June of 2004, and it was so warm that we would go up to the flying bridge of our boat in the early evening to have our gin and tonics in the shade! Only when the sun went over the mountain did it get cool enough to cook!

In the early 1970s several remote old farms in this area became counter culture homesteads for Americans seeking a quieter lifestyle away from the worry of getting drafted into the army and sent to Vietnam. I was exploring this area with my girlfriend in a small sailboat in the summer of August of 1971, and anchored in remote Galley Bay. Among the old apple trees rising up from the shore were what appeared like yurts and geodesic domes. We were sitting enjoying a glass of wine when there was a commotion in the water off our stern and there was this exquisite young woman, swimming nude, and wondering if we could spare any cigarettes!

There are few things better than exploring around one of the anchorages here by small boat on a still summer morning. In several places there are rope swings on overhanging trees —perfect for swinging out and dropping into the deep water!

Top: Looking northeast towards the coastal mountains from the entrance of Desolation Sound. The steep and inhospitable terrain ended Vancouver Islanders' dream of a railroad that would loop around Desolation Sound and bridge Seymour Narrows.

51

Don't Miss Seymour!

Oosterdam in Seymour Narrows, just about to pass over the exact spot where Ripple Rock was blasted out of the middle of the channel. Several cubic miles of water must pass through this channel every few hours as the tide rushes in and out, creating very swift currents. Safe passage through the Narrows is only possible near the times of high or low tide.

Once I was in the wheelhouse of a Princess ship transiting the Narrows, and I wondered how much water we acrually drew as we passed over where Ripple Rock used to be. "36 feet," came the terse answer...Thinking for a moment, I realised that at that stage of the tide, there was only 41 feet over the rock; so our bottom was passing within 5 feet of it; no wonder the Captain and pilot were a little tense.

"Hey, kid, wake up, ya gotta see this..!"

It was June, 1965, I was 18, had just left Seattle on my first Alaska fishing boat job, and the 70 year old mate woke me. I stumbled up into the wheelhouse, amazed at what I was seeing: great, slowly turning whirlpools, through which the skipper struggled, turning the wheel back and forth, trying to find a safe way between them.

"It used to be worse, before they blasted Ripple Rock!"

Along the waterfront, Seymour Narrows, **mile 205**, was a legendary place. A ship killer rock had lurked, right in the middle of the channel, creating whirlpools large enough to suck down good sized boats. Safe passage was only possible at slack water, near the times of low and high tide. For big ships, this was the only sheltered route north, and as they got bigger, "Old Rip" became more and more of a hazard.

First they tried drilling from a barge anchored with four **250 ton anchors!** Didn't work—the violent current meant that the drill bits kept breaking off.

Finally a huge drilling project was undertaken—over

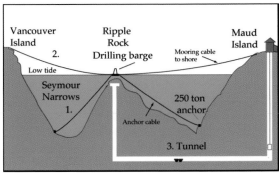

Top: drill barge positioned directly over Ripple Rock with the violent rapids generated by the two pinnacles that lurked just below the surface clearly visible. Because of the currents and whirlpools, drilling from the barge proved infeasible. Left: The tunneling project was only begun after it became clear that the swift currents made it impossible to blast the rock any other way.

3200' of tunnels and vertical shafts—reaching up into the interior of the rock. This was before the sophisticated sort of surveying equipment that we take for granted today was available, and drillers would explore with small diameter drills—until they broke through to the water. Then they'd plug the hole and use the information to create a 3D map of where they were.

Finally tugs pushed **bargeloads of dynamite**—2.8 million pounds to load into the cave they had excavated, and on April 7, 1958: Adios Ripple Rock!

Passenger Tip

Ships departing Vancouver usually transit Seymour late at night or early morning. If the time isn't announced, ask; even in the dim twilight it is a dramatic sight. Southbound ships headed for Vancouver usually transit early evening so you'll have a much better chance to view it..

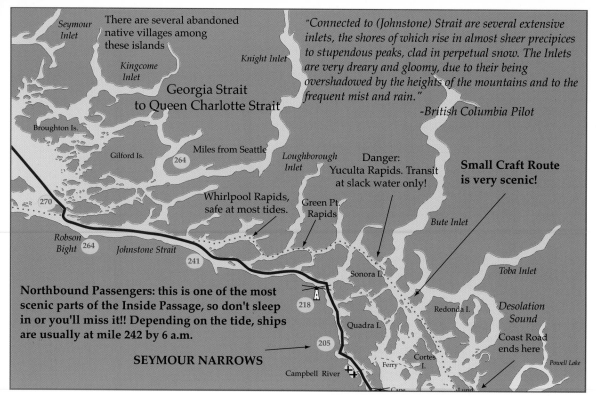

Seymour
Inlet

There are several abandoned native villages among these islands

Knight Inlet

Kingcome Inlet

Georgia Strait
to Queen Charlotte Strait

"Connected to (Johnstone) Strait are several extensive inlets, the shores of which rise in almost sheer precipices to stupendous peaks, clad in perpetual snow. The Inlets are very dreary and gloomy, due to their being overshadowed by the heights of the mountains and to the frequent mist and rain."
-British Columbia Pilot

Broughton Is.

Gilford Is.   Miles from Seattle

264

Loughborough Inlet

Danger: Yuculta Rapids. Transit at slack water only!

Small Craft Route is very scenic!

270

Whirlpool Rapids, safe at most tides.

Green Pt. Rapids

Bute Inlet

Robson Bight   264

Johnstone Strait

241

Sonora I.

Toba Inlet

Northbound Passengers: this is one of the most scenic parts of the Inside Passage, so don't sleep in or you'll miss it!! Depending on the tide, ships are usually at mile 242 by 6 a.m.

A

218

Quadra I.

Redonda I.

Desolation Sound

Coast Road ends here

205

SEYMOUR NARROWS

Cortes I.

Ferry

Powell Lake

Campbell River

Cape   Lund

Most large ships take the route marked by the blue line through this area. Smaller ships—say up to 225'—usually take the more winding and scenic route further east via Yuculta Rapids. Below: The old government dock at Shoal Bay is a good place to wait for slack water if you are south-bound through Yuculta Rapids.

--- Passenger Tip ---

Vancouver departing passengers: the area between Seymour Narrows, mile 205 and Pine Island, mile 319, is very scenic. If you sleep in, you'll miss it.

MAJOR LANDSCAPE CHANGES

Seymour marks a huge transition in your trip. Literally it is as if there were an invisible line that ran from just south of Seymour to just south of Yuculta Rapids. To the south is civilization—towns, roads, lights on the shore at night, a warmer climate.

The land to the north is very different—wilder, lonelier, cloudier, and chillier. This is the wild north coast where vast areas are sort of de facto wilderness, with here and there a logging camp, native village, or sportfishing resort, and the further north you go, the wilder it gets. Once you get north of Vancouver Island and into the channels and bays on the east side of Hecate Strait, you may find bays that go months without seeing a boat or a human.

The tide runs very swiftly through the Discovery Islands. There are a number of routes: Seymour for the big cruise ships, Yuculta Rapids for small cruise ships, yachts and fish boats (they like the narrow channels); and the narrowest channels in between, for even smaller craft, with crews willing to pick their ways through the rock piles.

Whatever the route, vessels must wait for slack water or close to it, for safe passage. To do otherwise risks getting capsized or swamped by the powerful whirlpools and rips.

"I was tied up to a log raft, up in Teakerne Arm, you know where it is, about 10 miles south of Yucultas, waiting for the tide. There was a Canadian salmon troller laying there, and the owner was out on the logs, so we visited for a bit. I was asking him about good places to duck in out of the weather if it got bad, and he knew some that I'd never heard of.

Then there was a sound from his boat, like a woman crying out, and he excused himself and walked back along the logs and disappeared into his boat. A long while passed with more crying, and then it got quiet and he came out again, wiping his hands on a rag. It looked like blood, so I asked him if every-thing was alright.

'Ah,' he said, 'that was the baby coming out.' He shrugged. 'A little girl. They're both fine.'"

- A B.C salmon troller

"It was thick o'fog, when we were waiting below the Yucultas 'fer slack, and we kept hearing something, like it was blowing, then they came up all around us—this pack o'killer whales—Jesus, there musta' been ten or twelve of them, with them big fins. Well sir, I want to tell ya', they waited and waited just like us, and then when that tide stopped running, they timed it just right and went through along with us, slack water, right on the button."

- A B.C. logger

Passenger Tip

Vancouver departing passengers: get up early! I know you are probably tired from your journey to the ship, but your ship will often transit this area early, so have your binoculars ready! Look for their noticeably tall dorsal fin and dramatic black and white coloring. This is also one of the more scenic areas along the Inside Passage.

Orca: Size: to 30 feet. Range: global, but especially coastal. Distinguishing features: bold black and white markings and dramatic tall dorsal fin on the male. Habits: Travels in extended family groups called pods, feeds on salmon, herring, marine mammals and other fish. Have been known to slide up onto ice floes to eat resting seals! Will also occasionally slide up on a beach with a breaking wave to grab an unwary seal, and try to wriggle off again in the next big wave.

It is almost as if nature set a gate across the route. At the very place where the busy south coast ends, and the wilderness begins. As if to warn the traveler of what lies beyond.

Johnstone Strait - mile 218 - 264 - is probably the best known place in North America to see orcas. The good months are July and August, when the orcas are chowing down on migrating salmon as well as seals which also eat the salmon.

British Columbia orcas played a huge part in the worldwide change in human perception and understanding of orcas. In June of 1965, Bill Lechkobit, a B.C. salmon fisherman caught a big bull orca in his net, near **Namu, mile 375**, and decided to try to keep it alive and sell it.

Seattle Aquarium owner Ted Griffin was very aware of the success that the Victoria Aquarium had with its captive orca, Moby Doll, and jumped at the opportunity to get one. He rushed up to Namu with a crew, built a floating underwater cage or pen, hired a tug, crossed his fingers and headed down to Seattle.

Griffin was very lucky, getting Namu safely to Seattle and installing him in a big tank in his aquarium with big viewing ports for the paying customers. As Moby Doll had in Victoria, Namu thrilled the customers, who quickly had to revise their perception of what an orca was.

Instead of an angry killer, audiences found a creature that was obviously intelligent, gentle, and even funny. National Geographic ran a 28 page story on Griffin and Namu that went a long ways to dispel the myths many had about orcas.

But just 11 months later Namu died from an infection. Griffin, devastated, realized what a money maker Namu had been for his struggling business and set out to capture another one.

Unfortunately all the publicity about Namu and Moby Dall created sort of a wild west gold rush mentality about capturing orcas, and Griffin captured a whole school of orcas on the east side of Whitbey Island, and offered them for sale. Tragically, in the commotion, several of the captured orcas accidentally died.

ORCA ALERT

This was not good publicity for folks who wanted to make a buck capturing orcas. Eventually the Washington state legislature became concerned and involved after an even more spectacular orca capture a few years later. This one occurred in an inlet so close to the actual capitol building in Olympia, Washington, that legislators could hear the helicopters! This was in the era of Earth Day and a swiftly growing awareness of the environment and the natural world, and shortly thereafter Washington, followed by British Columbia banned the capture of orcas. Unfortunately in the decade between Namu's capture and the bans, around 100 orcas were killed or taken from the Puget Sound-lower British Columbia orca population.

Orca awareness probably reached a peak after the release of "Free Willy,' starring an orca whose real name was Keiko. Poorly housed in a Mexican aquarium after the film, Keiko's plight inspired a large number of supporters, and his life became an astonishing saga of high profile fund raising by schoolchildren all over the world up to millionaires like Craig McCaw, an interim home in an custom made Oregon aquarium tank, and eventually a high profile ride in a U.S. Air Force C-17 transport and finally to the fjord in Iceland, near where he had been captured some 25 years earlier. There had always been an element of worry if he could be successfully reintroduced into the wild after so long in captivity. He was released successfully in the wild, where he survived for about 18 months before dying of pneumonia. At 27, he was old for a captive orca, but young for a wild one, many of whom live for 40 years plus.

The classic orca shot—a trio of big males in Johnstone Strait. If you are a passenger leaving Vancouver in July and August, try to get up early when your ship is transiting this part of the coast, as most ships will transit this area around daybreak. If you're southbound, you pass here in the afternoon, so you have a better chance to see one. Frans Lanting, Minden Pictures
Below: Orcas are a ubiquitous cultural symbol all throughout the Pacific Northwest.

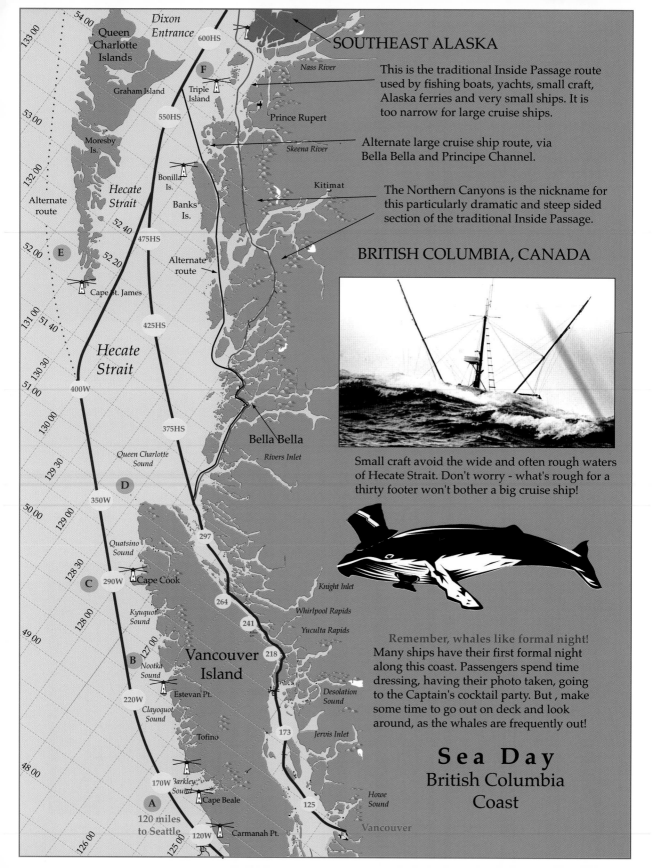

SOUTHEAST ALASKA

This is the traditional Inside Passage route used by fishing boats, yachts, small craft, Alaska ferries and very small ships. It is too narrow for large cruise ships.

Alternate large cruise ship route, via Bella Bella and Principe Channel.

The Northern Canyons is the nickname for this particularly dramatic and steep sided section of the traditional Inside Passage.

BRITISH COLUMBIA, CANADA

Small craft avoid the wide and often rough waters of Hecate Strait. Don't worry - what's rough for a thirty footer won't bother a big cruise ship!

Remember, whales like formal night! Many ships have their first formal night along this coast. Passengers spend time dressing, having their photo taken, going to the Captain's cocktail party. But, make some time to go out on deck and look around, as the whales are frequently out!

Sea Day
British Columbia Coast

Dixon Entrance

Queen Charlotte Islands

Graham Island

Nass River

Triple Island

Prince Rupert

600HS

550HS

F

Moresby Is.

Hecate Strait

Skeena River

Kitimat

Bonilla Is.

Banks Is.

Alternate route

475HS

E

Cape St. James

Alternate route

425HS

Hecate Strait

400W

375HS

Queen Charlotte Sound

Bella Bella

Rivers Inlet

D

350W

297

Quatsino Sound

C

290W Cape Cook

Kyuquot Sound

264

Knight Inlet

Whirlpool Rapids

241

Yuculta Rapids

Vancouver Island

B

127.00

Nootka Sound

218

220W Estevan Pt.

Clayoquot Sound

Desolation Sound

173

Jervis Inlet

Tofino

A

170W Barkley Sound

Cape Beale

125

Howe Sound

120 miles to Seattle

120W Carmanah Pt.

Vancouver

ALONG THE WAY - BRITISH COLUMBIA COAST

A Barkley Sound-Broken Islands area: wild and extremely rugged, accessed via settlement of Bamfield on eastern shore. The road to Bamfield itself is also very rugged; many visitors prefer to come by steamer from Port Alberni. Before about 1975, usually only visited by commercial fishermen and loggers. In recent years the Broken Islands, a mini archipelago of over 100 islands, and part of the Pacific Rim National Park, has become a major attraction for sea kayakers from all over the world. For the well-heeled, there are outfitters providing guided expeditions with the guides putting up the tents and cooking up the meals. Many prefer it the old-fashioned way: putting in at Bamfield, loading up with tents and supplies and exploring the islands on their own.

B Friendly Cove, Nootka Sound: In March of 1778 came the watershed event that was to change the coast forever: the arrival of the Europeans. British Captain James Cook arrived on his remarkable voyage of Pacific exploration, the very first wave of a tide of exploration and settlement that inadvertently decimated the native population through disease.

C Cape Cook: At the very western end of the Brooks Peninsula, this has traditionally been a difficult cape for small craft to round. More than one sailing couple with round-the-world ambitions, has abandoned further ocean sailing after a bad time at Cape Cook!

D Triangle Island: The British Columbia government had big plans for the 600' cliff here—the highest and brightest lighthouse on the entire coast, commissioned in 1910. Unfortunately they hadn't planned on the wind. The lightkeeper's dog blew off the cliff, and one storm blew the radio towers away and moved the office off its foundations against the generator building. Another storm blew the roof off the bunkhouse and the crews' clothes and bedding out into space. After just 8 years, the light was abandoned. Today, however, it is a major bird rookery. Each spring some 50,000 pairs of tufted puffins arrive, each to lay and incubate a single egg!

E Ninstints: Part of the Gwaii Haanas-South Moresby National Park Reserve, this was the site of a major village of the Haida tribe. Early visitors found a line of large multi-family lodges, fronted by dramatic mortuary totems. Today weather has taken its toll and just a few rotting house frames and tilting and fallen poles remain. Cape St. James, 15 miles south, is usually the windiest place on the British Columbia coast.

F Tide Rips: The sea floor rises at the north end of Hecate Strait to within 100' of the surface. In winter, when southerly storms are opposed here by flooding tides from the north, a violent tide rip can form, with seas big enough to threaten vessels as large as 100'.

Top: each summer native paddlers work their way up and down the coast to gatherings at different native villages. Above: in the inside waters of the BC coast, logs are moved from forest to mill in the traditional flat rafts like these. Towing these rafts is a tedious business as progress is slow and maneuvering is awkward.

In God's Pocket

Fishing boats waiting for weather, God's Pocket, Mile 310, June 1975. This very protected cove is the traditional 'jumping off place' for the often rough crossing of Queen Charlotte Sound. From my log that fall:

Oct 24:
"1230 - Egg Is. - sloppy, SE 20
1320 - Cape Caution, SE 25, 4' chop, wet going.
1500 - Pine Island - gale warning, wind here SE 40-45, very shitty going, had to tack downwind so as not to take seas on the beam.
1715 - God's Pocket - no room - full of Canadian trollers, laid alongside one fellow to fix our steering wheel.
1830 - Finally anchored, very narrow spot at SE end of Browning Pass. Steady 45 outside, water all white, glad to be inside!
Oct 25:
0845 - Underway on clearing, fresh morning. Little sleep last night; re-anchored twice and big Canadian troller drug down on top of us at 1 a.m. Wind and rain <u>very</u> violent all night.

Most Alaska-bound large cruise ships take a route just east of Hanson Island into Blackfish Sound, then George Passage and thence into the much wider waters of Queen Charlotte Strait. The area around mile 270—between Hanson and Harbledown Islands is particularly scenic, plus you can usually see the current swirls in the water from the tide here. Unfortunately northbound vessels often transit here early—7 a.m. or earlier, so you'll need to be an early riser to see it! Fortunately southbound vessels pass in the late afternoon to early evening.

Occasionally big ships might stop briefly in front of **Alert Bay**. This town, whose economic base is commercial fishing, is also the main center for native culture in the Johnstone Strait area. Your ship will probably get close enough for you to see the classic longhouse style buildings of the **U'mista Cultural Center,** and, if you look above town, you'll see what might look like a cell phone tower, but actually it is the **world's tallest totem pole**, 173' feet tall. At the opposite end of the waterfront from the cultural center is the **Namgis Burial Ground** with another noticeable collection of totem poles.

Look for the **Pine Island Lighthouse at mile 319**. If your route will go up straight up boring Hecate Strait, your ship will slow here to discharge (or receive, southbound) the Canadian pilots, who work with the navigational staff to guide the ship though the tricky channels inside of Vancouver Island.

Lighthouse families, particularly at Pine Island and the

Passing Bella Bella

next lighthouse to the north, equally exposed Egg Island, did not have an easy life. A 50' wave from a 1967 winter gale smashed most of the buildings here and the staff with their children huddled by a campfire on higher ground until the storm had passed. Another storm smashed the Egg Island keeper's house into kindling; they were lucky to survive until help arrived.

For all smaller vessels traveling up the BC coast, this section—Queen Charlotte Sound—was almost always the most challenging, as it was open waters, exposed to the wind, a 40 mile 'crossing' between the shelter of a cove nicknamed God's Pocket on the south and Safety Cove on the north.

Your route in Hecate Straits usually pretty much runs up the middle of the strait. You may see the snow covered 10-11,000' tops of the coast mountains to the east, and you may see some lower land to the west.

This would be the **Queen Charlotte Islands**, among the most rugged and thinly settled of the B.C. coast. They were originally settled by the Haidas, a First Nation tribe, who suffered the same ravages from disease and alcoholism as their mainland brothers. The islands are becoming favored by kayakers and adventure travelers seeking a true off the beaten path experience. Guides stress the remoteness of the land, and the importance of carrying adequate survival equipment and leaving a travel plan with a friend at home in case you don't return on schedule.

Dawn Princess passing Dryad Point, mile 400 on a 2006 voyage. Consider yourself lucky if your ship takes this route. Years ago, most ships took these winding channels, but in recent years, as ships got bigger, the tendency was to take the wider, safer, more direct (but only by a few miles) route up Hecate Strait. But it is definately more boring. There is some Captain discretion here; ask yours if he'd take your ship through Lama Passage.

--- Passenger Tip ---

Don't feel you have to eat dinner in the big formal dining rooms. Explore your ship, particularly the buffet areas. Many are up the bow with 180 degree views, some even segregate part for white tablecloth, waiter served dinners. (Sometimes you have to pay extra.) But consider the view: you can go out to an elegant restaurant anytime, but how often do you get to eat dinner with the coast of British Columbia or Alaska passing by?

Above: a big oceangoing raft being constructed on the Columbia River, circa 1920. Davis rafts used to transport logs from the Queen Charlotte Islands were similar. The traditional flat style of log raft was not suited for the rough waters of Hecate Strait.
OHS 7863/11436

A distinctive, Haida mortuary style totem, usually carved to honor a deceased chief, whose ashes are sometimes put in a cavity on the back.

Thirty miles west of **mile 480W** is **Skedans**, once the side of a large Haida village, now abandoned, but site of many old totems and other artifacts. It is a United Nations World Heritage Site.

From about 1910 to 1941, several whaling stations operated out of the Queen Charlottes, harvesting the schools of humpback, finback, sperm, and even the giant blue whales that migrated up and down the coast. It was hard, hard work with crude navigational equipment on an unforgiving coast.

Commercial fishing, logging, and a bit of tourism are pretty much the economic base of these islands. Most of the logs cut here are transported to mills at Prince Rupert or on Vancouver Island for processing. In the inlets and passages between Vancouver Island and the mainland, the waters are sheltered enough for the traditional flat log rafts. However, this sort of raft could not stand the rigors of the rough ocean conditions of Hecate Strait, so an alternate raft design was developed, with hundreds of thousands of board feet of logs chained tightly together tightly enough to survive rougher conditions. Eventually big barges were used, complete with cranes to allow them to load themselves in remote inlets. With the addition of ballast tanks that could be flooded or pumped out as needed, these barges became self dumping as well. They'd get towed to their destination. Then the tanks on one side would be emptied and the barge would tip all the logs into the water!

Whale Ho!

The islands suffered a hard blow in March of 2006, when their regular ferry, the *Queen of The North* hit an island in the middle of a rainy, windy night and sank. Fortunately a few fishermen at a nearby First Nations village were awake with their radios on and immediately headed out in their boats to rescue the survivors, who were shivering in life rafts. Two passengers were lost in the confusion of the sinking.

If you are northbound, this will usually be a formal night. Couples will spend time getting dressed; perhaps the ladies might get their hair done. Then there is the Captain's cocktail party as well as the all-important formal portrait.

Don't forget this is whale country as well. Today most ships carry naturalists who have a beeper. If the bridge staff spots a school of whales, they would often page the naturalist to come up to the bridge to do a running commentary. But if it's just one whale, and if an announcement would interrupt an important passenger activity, it might not be announced. Many times in Hecate Strait, I've been walking the deserted outside decks and spotted whales, seeming eager for attention, while almost everyone else was inside, occupied with formal night activities.

So... remember to take time in your busy afternoon to take a stroll on the outer decks—the promenade decks on most ships are sheltered from the wind—and keep a sharp eye peeled for whales.

The Alaska border is at **mile 604**, but it is a lonely windy place, far from any town, usually passed by big cruise ships in the middle of the night with little fanfare.

Passenger Tip

Remember, Hecate Strait is whale country. There is a lot going on board your ship the first day out of Vancouver, but don't forget to keep a eye out for humpbacks. Look for the distinctive puff of what looks like smoke as they surface and exhale.

Humpback Facts

Size: 30' to 50', weight to 40 tons. Range: oceanic, cooler waters like British Columbia and Alaska in the summer, and warmer, like Hawaii, in the winter. Distinguishing features: black with white throat or belly, long flipper with irregular edges. Knobs and bumps on head and flippers. Likes to breach or jump dramatically. Most common big whale along the northwest coast.

Salmon troller near Work Island, Mile 438, in Fraser Reach. A boat this size, traveling daylight hours, will take about a week to travel from Seattle to Ketchikan. Below: Two floating fishing lodges being towed to their summer locations. Because of the challenges of maintaining lodges in remote locations, lodges on barges are becoming popular, as after the season they can be towed to a town for the winter. Opposite top: Grenville Channel, near Mile 515—the narrowest part of the Inside Passage.

When cruise ships were small, say 300' feet and smaller, everyone pretty much took the traditional Inside Passage route, also nicknamed The Northern Canyons, instead of traveling up wide and sometimes windy Hecate Strait. The Northern Canyons begin at **Boat Bluff Lighthouse, Mile 439**. The next hundred miles or so are among the most spectacular of the whole Inside Passage. The walls of the channels seem to rise vertically in places and waterfalls tumble down their flanks. In places there is not enough room for two ships to pass.

This region was especially popular with hand loggers because of the steepness of the slopes which made it easier for the men who worked alone or with a single partner, to slide the huge trees down into the water.

If you take this route, look for **Butedale Cannery**, on the west side of Fraser Reach at **Mile 473**, a traditional stopping spot for fishing boats. Once a complete little town all by itself, with neat rows of houses for administrators and their families, and bunkhouses for hundreds of workers, it was all powered by water from the lake in the hills behind it. Sadly, after the canning operations were transferred to Prince Rupert, the large cannery fell into disrepair and, now, like many old North Coast canneries, lies abandoned.

AT THE BISHOP BAY HOT SPRINGS

In the windy fall of 1982, my crew and I were headed down the Inside Passage after a long and tiring four months of buying salmon all over Southeast Alaska and delivering them to the Icicle Seafoods cannery in Petersburg. The summer had been cold and rainy and the seas rough. Seeking a little R&R in that lonely stretch of coast, we steamed 15 miles up a narrowing side channel and tied to the roughly made ramp at the Bishop Bay Hot Springs. The only man-made structure in thousands of square miles of wilderness, it was a simple cinder block building over a pool in the rocks filled with hot water and a washing pool outside.

As we sat up to our necks in the steaming water, the aches and cares of a long season in The North seemed to fade away. Many miles from the nearest settlement, it was a favorite with yachtsmen and weary southbound Alaska fishermen.

We were lucky; that mid-October afternoon we were totally alone and we savored it.

Then there was a sound, and we looked out the windows to see a single humpback whale lifting his tail high in the air and then it was gone.

It was magic.

PRINCE RUPERT, B.C.

Before the Grand Trunk Pacific Railway punched a line down through the coast mountains to connect interior Canada to the sea at Prince Rupert, Port Essington, a cannery town on the Skeena River, eight miles south, was the business center of northern British Columbia,

The railroad totally changed things. It was the first place north of Vancouver where a direct line from interior Canada reached the sea, and almost immediately exports, particularly grain and timber poured out, and imports from Asia came in. Having the railroad made "Rupert" (as it is known locally) a cheaper place to process fish as well. As fish runs declined, and refrigerated tenders—fish buying & transport vessels—made it possible to bring fish from remote areas in to Rupert, the outlying canneries eventually closed and most north coast salmon were processed here. Today, Port Essington, once a booming town with several canneries, is a ghost town and Rupert is the regional center.

Sadly, Charles Hays, manager of the GTPRR, whose vision of Prince Rupert as a major port, never got to see his dream fulfilled. Returning from England where he had raised capital for the rail line through the mountains, he unfortunately chose to travel on the *RMS Titanic*. He was lost along with many, many others when it grazed

an iceberg that sliced the magnificent ship open and sent it to the bottom.

Today Prince Rupert's economy is like much of Southeast Alaska's was a few decades earlier: essentially dependent on commercial fishing and pulp mill employment, although port operations are a major employer as well.

Sensing the crowding of Southeast Alaska ports, and wanting to further diversify its economy, a modest cruise ship dock and terminal was completed in 2006, and a few ships began to schedule stops there.

A few blocks west of the new dock is the **Museum of Northern B.C.** with excellent displays on local First Nations culture and local history. A short walk away in downtown, behind the courthouse are the **Sunken Gardens.**

Today, almost all of all the hundreds of remote outlying canneries up and down the B.C. and Alaska coast are gone, abandoned or burned, most just pilings on a beach and buildings rotting in the forest. Fortunately at Prince Rupert, a group of concerned local citizens have preserved one, the old **North Pacific Cannery** on the Skeena River as a National Historic Site. Offered as an excursion to most visiting passengers, a visit is a remarkable glimpse into the past and a time when it seemed as if the salmon resource was, like the forest, endless. There's also a great local cafe—Smiles Seafood Cafe—with wonderful seafood if you are looking for a colorful eatery.

Opposite top: Loading logs aboard an Asian log ship; a good way to export jobs as well. Opposite lower: Inside the North Pacific Cannery, a National Historic Site, an aide explains the canning process. Top: A cannery tender tows sailing salmon gillnetters out out from the Skeena River, circa 1920. It's hard to believe, but at its peak, there were over 200 canneries operating in this area! Above: wheat car waiting to be unloaded. 'Rupert,' thanks to the railroad winding down the Skeena River Canyon, is a major port for western inland Canada.

Who was it who first brought smallpox, syphilis, and gonorrhea ashore to the natives? Was it Captain Cook's sailmaker, Captain Vancouver's gunner, an American whaler, a Spanish trader? It mattered little. A plague worse than that which swept Europe in the Middle Ages raced up and down the coast in the decades after the whites arrived.

But before the first contact natives along this coast enjoyed the fruits of a prosperous and successful culture. And the key was simply this: The sea and the forest provided. The early white settlers had a saying for the bounty of the sea: when the tide was out the table was set.

First of all, as compared to much of the rest of North America, the climate was mild. Mighty cedar trees provided wood for housing, for canoes, bark for clothing and baskets. The sea was full of crab, halibut, herring, candlefish (they could actually be dried and burned) but especially the salmon, which could be caught in great numbers and dried and smoked for the winter.

Typical villages were large wooden multi family lodges, set near the beach of a protected cove. The natives traveled and traded up and down the coast in their long carved canoes, fought at times, but in general, lived in harmony with the land and, by the standards of the times, enjoyed a rich and prosperous culture.

Their wealth allowed them to create stunning works of art, in particular masks, generally used in ceremonial dances, and totem poles, used to record history in cultures without a written language.

But when the first sails of the European explorers appeared off the Northwest Coast starting in the 1750s, a curtain was about to be drawn on a powerful native culture that had endured for centuries.

By the 1890s or so, native culture was essentially collapsing, and spectacular works of art which had previously symbolized their greatness were rapidly disappearing into the forest as whole villages were first decimated by disease and then abandoned.

A Culture
Lost

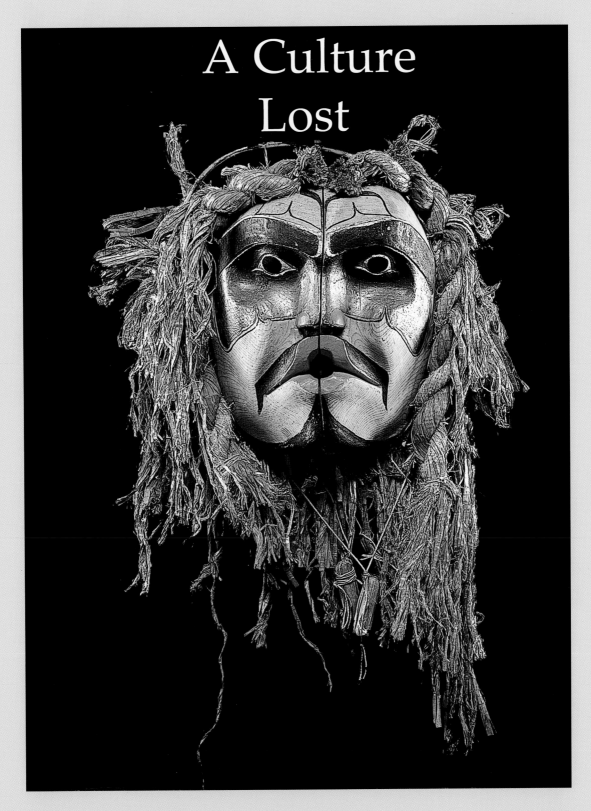

RAINFOREST NATIVE CULTURE
CIRCA 1900

Hidden in protected coves with long cedar canoes drawn up on the beach before them were the homes of a proud culture. The coming of the White Man was a double edged sword - they brought employment, typically in salmon canneries many miles from the natives' home villages - and a wide variety of trade goods.

But they also brought diseases to which the coastal natives had no immunity, and alcohol which created a whole other disease.

The result was that within a few decades, native populations had collapsed up and down the coast and whole villages like Tanu, top, had been abandoned. Photo credits All AMNH: Opposite page: 42298, 46104, 42263. This page: 248614, 44310.

Hidden in the woods of Tongass Island, near the southern Alaskan border with Canada, an old totem slowly disintegrates into the forest. An hour's search on hands and knees on the beach in front yielded tiny but brightly colored glass trading beads, thrown into the sea, a native told us, as an offering to the gods for a safe canoe journey.

Very fortunately, collectors from the great museums of Europe and the East Coast were aware of the situation and came to the Northwest Coast to buy and salvage what they could. And they found a truly remarkable man to help them: George Hunt. His dad was the manager of the Hudson Bay Trading Post in a big native village; he grew up surrounded by Kwakiutl culture, married the daughter of an influential chief, had an intimate knowledge of native traditions, and was a trusted member of the Kwakiutl community. He was able to lead the collectors deep into the island wilderness to the most remote villages, to collect the stunning pieces of art that are all that remain from that era. Much fine art simply disappeared into the forest as village after village was abandoned, destroyed by the twin scourges of disease and alcoholism.

In the 1920s and 30s and 40s, boaters here would come upon evidence of a disintegrating culture - whole villages abandoned with the big lodges standing empty, being reclaimed by the forest. Today native guides live at the old sites to protect them and share with visitors the history of their powerful culture that once ruled the coast, but was swept aside by disease.

Today, native culture is more prosperous, thanks to fishing, logging, and government programs. Many tribes have their own museums, and the legacy masks and other art is slowly being returned to their rightful owners. Today coastal natives - called First Nations in Canada - live in modest communities called reserves among the coastal islands. As in Alaska, their economy is a combination of state provided social services, and income from logging, commercial fishing, and in Alaska, income from tribal investments.

FROM A TRAVELER'S JOURNAL, 1930s:

"We lifted the long bar from the great door of a community house, and stood, hesitating to enter. In the old days a chief would have greeted us when we stepped inside–a sea otter robe over his shoulder, his head sprinkled with white bird down, the peace sign. He would have led us across the upper platform between the house posts, down the steps into the center well of the house. Then he would have sung us a little song to let us know we were welcome, while the women around the open fires beat out the rhythms with their sticks. The earth floor would have been covered with clean sand in our honor, and cedar bark mats hastily spread for our sitting. Slaves would have brought us food - perhaps roe nicely rotted and soaked with fish oil.

"Sunlight and darkness, heat and cold, in and out we wandered. All the houses were the same size, only the house posts distinguished them. Some were without wallboards, some were without roof boards- all were slowly rotting, the remains of a stone age, slowly dying."
                                                              - M. Wylie Blanchet, *The Curve of Time*.

GEORGE HUNT: STRADDLING TWO WORLDS

"Sometimes while we are sleeping my wife would start up and sing her PExEla (Shaman) songs. Then while she stop singing, she would talk to the spirit and she seems to get answer back. Next time spirit comes to her I will write what she say to it."

- George Hunt in *Chiefly Feasts,* edited by Aldona Jonaitis

Deeply steeped in Kwakiutl and coastal native traditions, George Hunt was in a unique position among whites on the coast when the collectors from the big Eastern and European museums started coming to the coast in the late 1800s. Not only was he married into a native (or First Nations) family, but he himself had a deep appreciation for native culture and traditions. In addition, he had a clear sense of where some of the best art was located and was able to both lead the collectors to those remote locations - often by dugout canoe - and was also able to arrange purchase. AMNH 32734

THE NOOTKA WHALER'S WASHING SHRINE

After the major collecting expeditions to the Northwest Coast were over, George Hunt continued to pursue unusual pieces of art, hearing, in his travels of an unusual sculpture in Nootka. In order to even access the site, he had to assure the chief of the Nutkas that he was a shaman. So to test Hunt's claim the chief brought in a sick native for him to heal. Fortunately the man healed on his own, but the credit went to Hunt and he was allowed to visit the sacred site.

According to Nootka legend, centuries ago a shaman named Tsaxwasap inherited a small shrine consisting of several skulls and some hemlock branches, and knew that if he could somehow kidnap infants and skulls, the shrine would attract whales for the Nootka whalers. He started off by kidnaping ten newborns, the necessary skulls, plus twelve dried-up corpses, and magically the shrine began attracting many whales to the thankful Nootkas. Over time the corpses rotted away, to be replaced with wooden carvings.

The American Museum of Natural History was thrilled to see the photos like the one above that Hunt sent and authorized Hunt to buy it, hoping to re erect the shrine within the museum.

But when Hunt tried to make a deal, two chiefs each claimed ownership. Eventually, Hunt made a deal: $250 to each chief plus some of the Kwakiutl Cannibal Society songs that Hunt had collected. But, the deal also was that Hunt had to come and get everything at night.

Sadly, the Shrine was never erected, the Museum felt it would take up too much room. So this elegant tableau sits in storage, while the descendants of the Nootka are trying to get it back.

AMNH 104478. Opposite AMNH 16/771

A Man In A Boat Could Travel For Weeks and Never Find a Town

The coast, like British Columbia, is deeply indented with inlets winding back into a mountainous and forbidding interior. The islands, large and small, form a maze of channels. In the northern part, glaciers lie at the head of most of the inlets discharging ice year round.

A vast part of the area is thickly forested, without settlements or towns, little changed since the arrival of white men. Almost all the land is owned by the Federal Government and little is available to individuals.

There are a few towns, none large. Each has a few miles of roads, but for the most part, they aren't connected to each other and travel between is by boat or plane.

Scattered in little coves and harbors far from the towns are a few roadless fishing communities that still enjoy a quieter existence. Except for the storekeepers and the fish buyers, the residents mostly fish for salmon. In summer they are scattered - from the bay in front to up and down the coast. Summer is a busy time - with boats from far and near, hustling to make a year's pay in a few short months.

But then comes the fall - the outside boats straggle back to Washington State, and by the first of November, the locals are pretty much tied up for the winter. The days get short, the sun disappears between thick clouds. Weeks might pass with only the mail boat or a float-plane setting down to break the monotony.

Despite the short days and the gloomy weather, many of the local residents prefer the winter. Salmon season is a rush, and winter can be a welcome change, with time to work on cabin or boat, visit with neighbors, or just sit and read. It's not a fast paced life, but there's enough to do to just keep going. Many of the residents have spent time in the larger towns and wouldn't think of moving back.

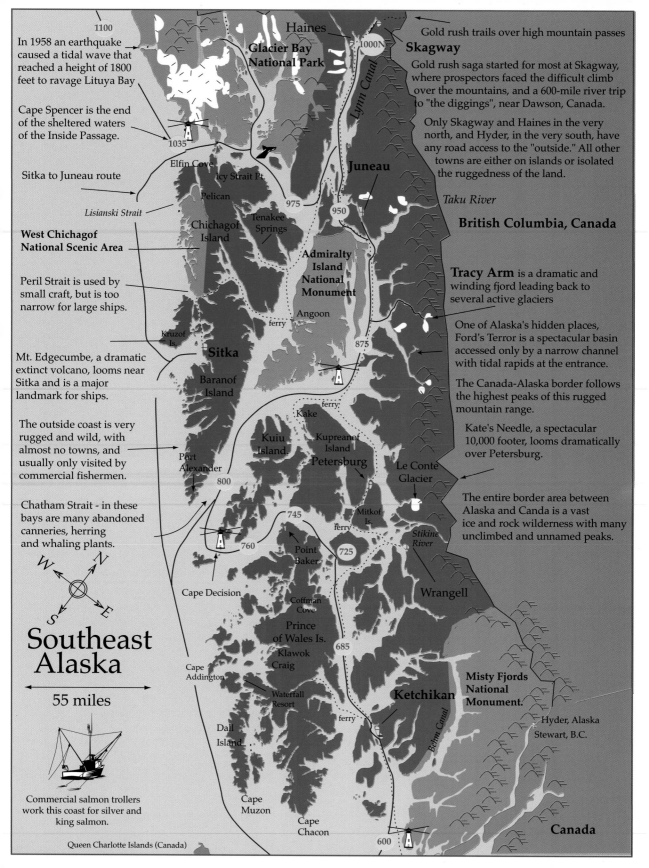

In 1958 an earthquake caused a tidal wave that reached a height of 1800 feet to ravage Lituya Bay

Cape Spencer is the end of the sheltered waters of the Inside Passage.

Sitka to Juneau route

West Chichagof National Scenic Area

Peril Strait is used by small craft, but is too narrow for large ships.

Mt. Edgecumbe, a dramatic extinct volcano, looms near Sitka and is a major landmark for ships.

The outside coast is very rugged and wild, with almost no towns, and usually only visited by commercial fishermen.

Chatham Strait - in these bays are many abandoned canneries, herring and whaling plants.

Southeast Alaska

55 miles

Commercial salmon trollers work this coast for silver and king salmon.

Gold rush trails over high mountain passes

Skagway

Gold rush saga started for most at Skagway, where prospectors faced the difficult climb over the mountains, and a 600-mile river trip to "the diggings", near Dawson, Canada.

Only Skagway and Haines in the very north, and Hyder, in the very south, have any road access to the "outside." All other towns are either on islands or isolated the ruggedness of the land.

Taku River

British Columbia, Canada

Tracy Arm is a dramatic and winding fjord leading back to several active glaciers

One of Alaska's hidden places, Ford's Terror is a spectacular basin accessed only by a narrow channel with tidal rapids at the entrance.

The Canada-Alaska border follows the highest peaks of this rugged mountain range.

Kate's Needle, a spectacular 10,000 footer, looms dramatically over Petersburg.

The entire border area between Alaska and Canda is a vast ice and rock wilderness with many unclimbed and unnamed peaks.

Haines

Glacier Bay National Park

1100

1035

Elfin Cove

Icy Strait Pt.

Pelican

Lisianski Strait

Chichagof Island

Tenakee Springs

975

950

1000N

Juneau

Admiralty Island National Monument

Angoon

ferry

875

Kruzof Is.

Sitka

Baranof Island

Port Alexander

800

Kake

ferry

Kuiu Island

Kupreanof Island

Petersburg

Le Conte Glacier

760

745

Point Baker

725

ferry

Mitkof Is.

Stikine River

Cape Decision

Wrangell

Coffman Cove

Prince of Wales Is.

685

Klawok Craig

Cape Addington

Waterfall Resort

ferry

Ketchikan

Misty Fjords National Monument.

Hyder, Alaska

Stewart, B.C.

Dall Island

Behm Canal

Cape Muzon

Cape Chacon

600

Canada

CHAPTER 3

Islands Without Number:
Alaska Border to Juneau

"Gazing from the deck of the steamer, one is borne smoothly over calm blue waters, through the midst of countless forest-clad islands. The ordinary discomforts of a sea voyage are not felt, for nearly all the whole long way is on inland waters that are about as waveless as rivers and lakes. So numerous are the islands that they seem to be sown broadcast; long tapering views between the largest of them open in every direction."

- John Muir, *Travels in Alaska*

In Southeast Alaska, the size of some small states, thousands of islands are divided by tide swept channels. To the east the border runs along the highest peaks of the coastal range; to the west the North Pacific Ocean beats on a rugged coast with just a single town: Sitka.

The land is not friendly. The forest starts right at the water's edge and is almost impenetrable. In the roadless communities residents often find it easier to take an outboard skiff over to a neighbors just a hundred yards away rather than brave the spiny devils club and thick undergrowth in the forest.

In summer, the days are long, sunlight often until ten or

Top: Ketchikan waterfront: in a country of mostly water and islands, the floatplane and the outboard are indispensable. Below: A wet day along the waterfront, Southeast Alaska. But let's face it, despite all the little jokes about liquid sunshine, etc., Southeast Alaska, with an average annual rainfall of 152 inches (Seattle, at 36 inches, is considered rainy...) can be, as Ketchikan artist Ray Troll puts it, "as close as you can get to actually living underwater..."

AFOGNA

Top: tender or fish buying boat, unloading totes of iced fish, while a heavily loaded salmon seiner waits its turn. Though cruise passengers may see little evidence of it, commercial fishing is still a major economic engine all throughout Alaska. Below: while their family boat unloads, the sons hang out with the dog...

eleven at night near the June summer solstice. People stay up, working or fishing, 16,18, 20 hours a day. But then comes the long winter with the sun over the mountain at 3 in the afternoon, not to reappear until 9 or so the following morning. And those are the hard days.

But even from the earliest days, it was a land that drew hardy people: fishermen, trappers, loggers, cannery workers, sawmillers, tugboaters, card sharks. And drinkers.

In the early days, most everyone made their living with their hands. As much as anything perhaps, this is what appealed to a certain type of people from 'down south,' or the 'lower 48.' That here was a land where if you were strong, and you worked hard, you could make your place. Single men, with perhaps not much to recommend them except for maybe a certain bullheaded strength would say goodbye to friends and family and 'head up North.' Then maybe a few years later they'd stop back home again, obviously a modest success from their labors 'up North,' and maybe looking for a bride, for as The North had many things in abundance that might attract a man, like fish, and trees, and land, women were not among them.

For much of the 20th century, the economy of Southeast Alaska had three elements - fishing, logging, and tourism.

It was a good mix, with the sawmills providing a good base of employment in the wintertime when fishing was pretty much over until spring. Then in summer all the towns would boom as seasonal workers for the canneries and fish boats would roll in for the fishing season. Starting in the 1970s, when the Japanese economy entered the high growth mode, prices paid to Alaska fishermen seemed to rise, sometimes even weekly. Fishermen had new boats built and shiny new pickups rolled around town.

Then the 1980s and early 1990s brought sort of a double whammy. After many years of allowing logging practices that were damaging salmon streams and fish production, the Forest Service drew up stricter rules and the big mills at Sitka and Ketchikan closed. Then the Japanese economy took a big tumble, taking fish prices down with them, and fishermen and processors quickly reigned in their spending.

Today in most of the coastal towns that a cruise passenger might see, tourism is pretty much the biggest game in town, (except for the capital, Juneau, with its many government jobs) and many residents hope for the return of the days when their economy was more balanced.

Top: somewhere on the North Coast, a logger walks carefully on big hemlock and Doug Fir logs, waiting for the tug that will tow it to a mill. UW 6560 Below: Ketchikan Logging show for visitors.

Top: Rain forest near Icy Strait Point, an old cannery converted to a cruise port. It looks like the land has been selectively cleared, Most rain forest isn't this easy to walk through. Below: And the land isn't friendly either - try walking through the coastal rainforest and you'll find it to be almost impenetrable, not to mention full of nasty Devil's Club.

There aren't any duty free shops clustered around this border: it's a lonely, windy spot, exposed to the wind, wracked by tidal currents. The prudent mariner hurries across.

Look for the high ridge of snow-covered peaks to the east. They effectively seal off Southeast Alaska from any land connection, except in the very north at Haines and Skidway, and tiny Hyder, pop. 100, far up Portland Canal. Fortunately the larger (population 500) town of Stewart, B.C. is just two miles away and residents can share shops and services. The 2001 movie, Insomnia, was filmed near here.

Study the map carefully here. This entire area, with many winding inlets that all had to be explored, was very difficult for Vancouver and his men.

In the 1920 and 30s, there were several canneries in this area, at Hidden Inlet and Nakat Inlet. Today the old canneries have pretty much disappeared into the forest, just leaving old pilings and rusty machinery on the shore, and the whole area is essentially wilderness, all part of the **Misty Fjords National Monument.**

Look for salmon gill-netters, typically fishing Sunday noon through Wednesday noon. If the weather is calm, you may also see fish packers (they're larger) making their rounds among the fleet, buying fish. Many vessels remain the summer here, remote from any town or cannery, getting water, groceries, fuel, and supplies from the tenders, or fish packers, that service the fleet.

Just a decade or so ago, fishermen would just throw their fish into their dry fish hold and deliver them at the end of the day. Today all Alaska salmon processors are working hard to improve the quality of their fish, and encourage their fishermen to ice their fish. To this end, a barge with a generator and an ice-making machine is usually anchored in Foggy Bay, Mile 622, to serve the fishermen in this area.

The salmon fishery in Alaska is huge - each season more than 3,000 salmon fishing boats work the vast Alaska coast. Many come up from the Puget Sound area as there actually aren't enough fishermen in Alaska to catch all the salmon. Some of these fishermen leave home with cases of jars of fruit and vegetables that their families have put up for them from the garden at home. With a typical fishing period of just three or four days a week, there's plenty of time on the weekends. Crab and salmon are so abundant here, that some fishermen will set up little processing operations aboard their boats and refill the same jars with crab and salmon to be consumed all winter!

Glass balls, prized by collectors, can occasionally be found on remote beaches. Note the etched pattern left by the netting on ball, middle row, left. Bottom glass float with grooved ends for attaching to a gillnet is quite a find.

ORCA TALES: AT LORD ISLANDS

One summer when my wife and I were running a fish buying boat on the Garnet Point run, we had an afternoon to explore the **Lord Islands, mile 602.**

We were possibly the only human visitors in decades. The islands were remote and tiny and there were far more sheltered anchorages just a few miles away.

And so wild! The trees were bent and sculpted by the winter storms, the underbrush thick as a wall, but with exquisite tiny beaches on the west sides. My wife and I could tell at once that it might be a good place to look for the highly sought after glass balls. We started onto the beach then stopped, not wanting to disturb the two obviously very young seal pups sunning just above the surf line.

Then as we watched, stunned, a big orca surfed in on a wave, headed like an arrow for the pups. He snatched one up with a single snap of his big jaws, as the other quickly wriggled further up the beach. Then, when the next big sea washed around him, the orca wriggled back into the water and disappeared. All this happened in less tha 30 seconds. Our mouths hung open; we were amazed.

Ketchikan

Salmon and Totem Pole Capital of Alaska

Don't be fooled by the restaurants and jewelry boutiques along the waterfront here; until relatively recently, this was a full on rough and tumble logging and commercial fishing town. Right where the cruise ships now tie up used to be a big sawmill and a three story smoky sawdust burner, and canneries, cold storages, and fish processors lined the waterfront. Fishing boats, headed up to Alaska from the lower 48, and bound for other parts of the remote Alaska coast would always stop here to let the crew wet their whistles. And the next morning the skipper would just hope that they all made it back aboard.

Saturday nights in those days were particularly rough. Out in the channel floatplanes would start to land, big twin-engine Grumman Geese, and the slow, lumbering Stinsons, bringing in loggers from Prince of Wales Island and Tsimshian Indians from the village of Metlakatla. Then the fishing boats - big seiners and tenders - would start to arrive from the outer districts, the crews with a few bucks in their ass pockets, ready for a big night, drinking and carousing at Dolly Arthur's and the other brothels along the boardwalk at Creek Street, known as the only place in Alaska where the fish and the fishermen both came to spawn.

The first whites arrived in the 1870 to salt salmon. Next, as the technology to put fish in cans was

Top: A purse seiner hauls the end of the net aboard with a good haul of pink salmon or "humpies." These handsome boats with their power blocks hanging from the ends of their booms and nets and big skiffs on their back decks are seen throughout the region. Dan Kowalski photo. Above: A bit of non- traditional art by native carver Stephen Jackson on a pole in front of the New York Hotel and Cafe Left: Detail on one of the many totem poles around Ketchikan.

developed, the first of many canneries were established, and Ketchikan became a primary fishing center.

The history of Ketchikan is deeply intertwined with the three major native tribes of the region, the Tlingits, Haidas, and Tsimshians. Natives traditionally fished commercially and worked in the canneries as well as the sawmills.

When the whites arrived, there were numerous native villages throughout the area, but over time some of these settlements were depopulated primarily because of the diseases that the first whites brought to the area.

Big industry came to town around 1950, in the shape of the big Ketchikan Pulp Company mill out at Wards Cove, eight miles north of downtown.

Conceived as a way to utilize some of the vast spruce and hemlock forests of the region, and generate good paying, year round jobs (most fish and fish processing jobs were seasonal) the mill got a sweet deal from the U.S. Forest Service, and quickly became the largest employer in town.

But by the 1960s and 70s, salmon fishermen began to complain that logging practices like driving bulldozers down the middle of salmon streams and indiscriminate clear cutting was reducing the salmon runs on which they depended. The mill operators wanted to cut when and how they pleased, were backed up by the Forest Service, and for years there was ill feeling between these two factions in town.

Eventually more responsible logging practices reduced the timber available to harvest and much to the surprise of its employees, the mill closed its doors in 1997. Today, a smaller plywood mill operates on Gravina Island, but employs just a fraction of what the big Louisiana Pacific owned mill did.

Top: Salmon cannery, circa 1920. Chinese crews were a main source of labor for many early canneries, with their own bunkhouse and messhall. MOHAI 16233 Sometimes if you poke around in the ruins of old canneries you can even find old opium bottles. Right: part of the old Ketchikan Pulp Company mill at Wards Cove, four miles west of downtown.

THE NEW ECONOMY

A few years after the mill closed, salmon prices took a big tumble as well when the economy of Japan, our largest seafood customer, hit the skids. This hit the coastal communities, where there was little work except for fishing and processing, very hard.

About the same time, the cruise industry was beginning a major expansion, building much larger ships, and building lodges and infrastructure to transport, entertain, and house their passengers after they left the ships. Within a few years major changes came to Ketchikan, Skagway, and Juneau, the major cruise ports, as entrepreneurs created new excursions to offer the many new visitors off the ships, as well as new shops. The rapid growth was not without its blemishes as Caribbean based chain jewelry stores began to drive smaller, local stores out of business. Additionally, the downtown shopping areas on the main streets that used to be primarily focused on services and products for locals became primarily oriented to visitors. These stores would close up quickly after the last ships of the season, leaving deserted streets with window after window, covered over with plywood for the winter.

Over time, many residents hope that economy that is more balanced between tourism, fishing, and timber will return to the region.

Ketchikan visitor to child:
  "How long has it been raining?
Child:
  "I don't know; I'm only five"

Top: Ketchikan waterfront, circa 1955. Logging, millwork, and fishing were pretty much the only games in town.
F. Garland Swain photo.

A fine early summer evening, 1982: my wife and I tied our 70 foot tender (a fish buying and mother ship to smaller fishing vessels) up at the float in Ketchikan to drop a passenger and stretch our legs.

We walked up the ramp and stopped. A big offroad pickup truck raised up on red shocks and knobby tires lurched to a stop at the one red light, stereo booming. The driver revved his engine loudly, rolled down his window and threw out a beer bottle that shattered on the street. The light changed, and with a squeal of his big tires, he disappeared around the corner toward cannery row.

Next, an obviously intoxicated older gentleman lurched uncertainly across the street toward the entrance to the Foc's'le Bar. But missed the door, walked straight into the wall next to it and collapsed into a pile on the sidewalk.

After fish buying in Misty Fjords, Saturday night Ketchikan seemed a bit rough. As we watched, a younger couple, hand in hand, walked down the street and settled on a bench on the dock, looking out at the evening light on the Narrows.

"At last," I remember thinking, "someone who's not drunk..." But then the man lurched for the woman, she resisted and they both fell off the bench to roll around on the broken glass and the dog shit on the dock.

We took our walk, but threw off our lines gladly a half hour later, plunging quickly into the wilderness archipelago that is Southeast Alaska.

HANNAH C

If there were one burr under Alaskan's saddles, spurring the push for statehood, it was the fish traps. Made of netting and hung from big log frames or from pilings, the traps caught migrating salmon. Alaskans deeply resented that the traps and canneries were mostly owned by distant Seattle companies.

Each trap had a watchman, often a tough, hard bitten Alaskan, but occasionally a green college kid. The fish pirates would approach the fish traps at night and threaten or, more commonly, pay off the watchman, and make off with a load of fish. Few Alaskans frowned on this, feeling that the Seattle-owned canneries were stealing their resource to start with.

> "The cannery told me to keep that kerosene lamp burning in the shack all night long, so it would look like I was awake; that sometimes kept fish pirates away. But that if push came to shove, they told me that it was better to let them have what they wanted instead of getting shot."
>
> - Fish trap watchman

Another way to steal fish was called "crick robbing" – the practice of fishing in closed areas, particularly the mouths of streams, where salmon often congregate by the thousands. To deter such robbing, "fish cops" patrol in boat and floatplane, and college students are often hired to camp on major salmon streams, count the fish going up, and deter creek robbers by their presence.

Top: Trap tender vessel 'brailing' the fish out of a floating fish trap. The traps kept the fish alive until the cannery needed them. THS photo. Bottom: Old pile driving scow, Waterfall Cannery, 1972. Big enough to house and feed a crew, these scows were busy each salmon season driving pilings and installing fish traps.

WALKING AROUND TOWN

The good thing about all the major towns in Southeast Alaska is that they're small and the ships usually tie up or lighter passengers ashore right in downtown.

In Ketchikan, there's plenty to see on foot within a few blocks of the ship, and lots of variety if you want to walk a little further, as well as regular city buses if your feet get too tired to walk back!

The big **Southeast Alaska Discovery Center** downtown has excellent historical exhibits, a bookstore, coffee shop, and theatre showing a free regular feature on native culture. Adjacent is The Great Alaska Lumberjack Show, highlighting loggers competing in axe work, tree climbing, etc.

Another block or so of walking takes you to Creek St., the old red light district, today transformed into one of the more unique and eclectic shopping and eating areas of

Top: Saxman native village is a must stop - feeling like a walk? It's just a two mile walk south from town. Left: the New Ketchikan - the Orca Mall right on the dock. Bottom: more great piling art...

Alaska. The creek was handy - in prohibition days, boot-leggers would slink up in the black of the night at high tide, paddle under the establishments, give the secret knock, and trapdoors would open and eager hands change cash for booze. A short walk to the north is the Tongass Historical Society, and to the east the Totem Heritage Center. On the left just before the bridge over the creek is an excellent bookstore, **Parnassus**.

A really nice two mile walk, one way, is along the waterfront to the south past cannery row and the Coast Guard Station to **Saxman**, a native village with an excellent collection of totem poles, a clan lodge with the Cape Fox Dancers performing when the ships are in, as well as a carving shed. Of the three totem pole collections around Ketchikan, I like Saxman the best, because it is in an actual native village, and one gets a true sense of the struggle to make it in a fishing and logging economy.

Also the walk along the shore is a great place to look for bald eagles and see how many of the waterfront places have a plane in their backyard. There is a city bus that stops at the bottom of the hill - schedule and fare posted inside the little tribal museum on the right just up the hill - if you want to rest your feet on the way back. If you are up for a longer walk, consider the trip up to Deer Mountain Trail, entrance near Creek St.

Back in town a good place to catch some lunch is the Westmark Cape Fox Lodge - take the tramway that operates from Creek Street. On a bluff just south of downtown, the dining room offers a dramatic vista of the busy waterways and islands in front of town. At sea level just south of Creek St, is the unpretentious New York Hotel and Cafe, looking out on the boat harbor and the cruise ships beyond.

Most of the galleries and gift shops are located between the tunnel on Front Street, and Creek St. If you walk along the waterfront to the north past the tunnel, you'll find plenty of authentic Alaska to look at, especially along the water side.

Take some time to look around at the boats in the small boat harbors on both sides of the downtown docks where the cruise ships tie up. On most of the US coasts, boats this size - 40' and under - would be mostly be used for day fishing, the crews returning home at night to sleep in their own beds. But in Alaska with the fishing grounds often many hours from the nearest town, these boats are homes for their crews - often couples, sometimes with young children, for months at a time.

IN MISTY FJORDS

Actually, all of the lower southeast mainland and islands of Southeast Alaska are part of the Misty Fjords National Monument, essentially a vast wilderness, with few visitors except in the summer.

Excursions to Misty are available both by boat and plane or a combination of both. The most frequently visited spots, like Rudyerd Bay to the right, are about three hours away by boat. So if you travel both ways by boat, you'll spend a lot of your day going back and forth. One option is to take the boat in and then fly out in a seaplane. In my view, this is a wise choice, allowing you to see the dramatic marine seascape in one direction and then getting up for a higher vista on the other leg. When the visibility is good, the view from a seaplane above Misty can be truly spectacular. It's busy in the summer with planes, kayakers, and cruise boats, but in the winter, it's pretty much deserted except for two or three boats that fish the deep inlets and fjords for crab, shrimp, and halibut. Imagine what a week's trip in that awesome country would be like for them, probably without seeing another boat the whole time.

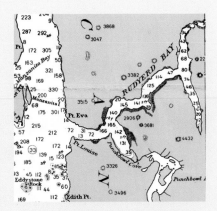

Opposite top: Waterfront statue, south end of cruise ship docks. Opposite bottom: Carver Nathan Jackson works in the totem shed at Saxman Native Village, a hour walk south of downtown.

Often flightseeing excursions will include landing on one of the mountain lakes or saltwater inlets to get an upclose look.

One morning over Misty

On a recent June morning, a friend picked me up at Ketchikan's Hotel New York at 4:30 a.m. for a flight over to Misty Fjords before the ships came in and the air got crowded. Perhaps because my friend had been an ER doctor in Ketchikan for more than a decade, he gave me a more detailed emergency briefing than any other floatplane pilot I'd traveled with. More than anything else, he focused on what to do if the plane flipped in a rough landing:

"First, you'll probably break at least one arm, so practise opening your seat belt and the door with your other hand... Remember the floats will be over your head, so don't hit them when you swim to the surface." Next, he had me practise with both hands turning around and getting the emergency air bottle out of the seat pocket behind me, good for 5 minutes breathing. Then he showed me how to push the button on the GPS emergency beacon, and repeated that my job was to get out, not to save him.

A few minutes later it was throttle up and we were rattling over the short harbor chop as we lifted off. 15 minutes later we were over the dramatic canyon that was Rudyerd Bay. No other planes, no cruise boats below yet - just us above that spectacular wilderness. We even had time to land on Punchbowl lake, climb up on the wing, and savor a hot coffee and a roll. Don't miss it!

Top right: We fly along 'The Wall,' at Punchbowl Cove. Left: Looking out toward Behm Canal from Smeaton Bay, on the usual flight excursion route. Above: the Pass Not Taken - on our return, we approached this pass in the hills on the way in to Ketchikan, but the cloud layer seemed to be dropping. Not wanting to find ourselves suddenly in the clouds with mountains all around us, we turned around. Good choice - there's a reason for the expression,"There are no old bold pilots..!" Top left: On the water at Punchbowl Lake, a popular spot.

Ketchikan Excursions

Just a sample - changes annually.
Misty Fjords - by air or sea, or a combination.
Bering Sea Fishermen's Tour (on vessel above)
Coastal Wildlife Cruise
Wilderness Exploration and Crab Feast
Sea Kayaking
Rainforest Wildlife Sanctuary Hike
Neets Bay Bear Watch and Seaplane Flight
Rainforest Ropes Course and Zipline Park
Bear Creek Zipline
Adventure Kart Expedition
Back Country Zodiak Expedition - U Drive
Flightseeing and Crab Feast
Totem Bight Park and Town Tour
Totem Bight and Lumberjack Show Combo
Saxman Native Village tour
Town and Harbor Duck Tour
Motorcycle Tour (as driver
Sportsfishing Expedition
Sportsfishing & Wilderness Dining (of your catch!)
Alaskan Chef's Table
City Highlights Trolley Tour
Mountain Point Snorkeling Adventure
And, as they say, many more.....
   Important note: if the tours available through your cruise line or ship are sold out, often similar tours will be available on the dock near the ship.

Around Town

ONCE THEY LOGGED FOR TREES..

But today they log to entertain visitors... Logging is still active in Southeast Alaska forests, but at a much reduced level than before the huge mills at Sitka and Ketchikan closed. In the 1950s, 60s, and 70s, big logging camps operated on Prince of Wales and other islands, and carrying loggers and supplies was a major source of revenue for the air taxi companies whose bread and butter today is excursions for cruise ship passengers.

This was the Grand Prix of American logging - the size of the trees and the difficulty of logging them were more than the equal of the famously big woods and trees of coastal Oregon, Washington, and British Columbia. The traditional flat log rafts were a common sight along the waterways, and so many log bundles escaped from rafts in rough water that "Beach logging" was a regular source of income for numerous salmon fishermen in the winter.

Today, logging is primarily on native owned land and a few small parcels of Forest Service land.

Will I catch a fish? At each cruise port excursions offer opportunities to go out into the salt water after the wily salmon. Typically the boats are modern, comfortable cruisers with heated cabins, toilets, and able to take parties of up to six. Depending on the season and where the "bite" is, vessels may run an hour or more to get to the fish.

Most sports fishermen here like to target on king and silver salmon. Kings, running up to 60 pounds and larger, (if you catch a king over 50 pounds, it is a big event...) are generally caught from May through August with the best fishing generally in the first half of the season. Silvers run smaller, typically 6 to 12 pounds, and are available mid-June through September. Pink salmon, much smaller and less desirable to the sportsman, are primarily caught by net and canned.

If you're not experienced, don't worry, there are a lot of fish here, and charter skippers are quick teachers.

Remember, it's not all about the fish. As much as anything else, going out on a charter boat for a day is an opportunity to get out close and see, up close and personal, some of the most abundant marine life and most dramatic scenery you will find anywhere. Whales, dolphins and eagles are all common sights for the charter fishermen so bring your camera.

What to do with your fish? In all towns, services are available to freeze, smoke, store, and ship your fish.

Left page: Logging show, Ketchikan, Giant cedar and loggers, circa 1900. Top: Commercial salmon troller off Cape Addington, 60 miles W of Ketchikan. You wouldn't have wanted to be there that morning. Above: "Fish on!" with friend, Sitka, 2008.

A CLOSE CALL

One winter morning my wife and I waited on the dock at remote Point Baker for the floatplane that would take us to Ketchikan and our ride south: the Alaska State Ferry. Just before the plane passed overhead to line up for the approach into that narrow and steep sided cove, an outboard skiff dropped off a friend with a lot of gear: three big heavy duffles and large suitcase.

A few minutes later the plane coasted up to the dock and the pilot took a long unhappy glance at all the gear on the dock; in addition to my friend's stuff, my wife and I also had four heavy bags. "If I'd known it was three 'o you guys, I'd have brought the Beaver."

The DeHavilland Beaver with its powerful rotary nine cylinder engine was the workhorse of the coast and islands, able to carry a much heavier load than the Cessna 185, which the pilot had ridden in on. But such is a bush pilot's lot; and without another word, we loaded up. As we stepped in and pushed away from the dock, it was obvious we were overloaded: the floats were almost totally underwater. The pilot started up and we taxied up to the very head of the cove; he knew he needed every foot of the cove to get into the air before the nasty looking tide rip at the entrance, and didn't turn around until his wings were literally breaking small branches off trees as we swung around into the wind.

He throttled up, giving it all he had. But it was a long time before the plane even got up on step and began accelerating. In the right hand seat, I peered anxiously ahead as the nasty looking tide tip, with easily a five foot almost vertical chop got closer and closer. I could feel the anxiety in the cabin when with just a hundred yards to go, the pilot pulled back on the stick, and we reluctantly staggered into the air, only to sink back, and bang along the steepening chop. Then there was no more time - he pulled us up off the water, just enough to clear the waves, and for a long moment we hung there on that narrow edge between life and death. No one spoke, or it seemed to me, even breathed. If we dropped just feet, our floats would hit the steep wavetops and we'd flip. Then we gained those few critical knots of speed and began climbing.

Floatplane Excursions

Alaska is a bush pilot's dream. Rugged, with extensive remote and roadless areas, the floatplane pulled up behind a modest house is a common sight all throughout the state. As any cruise ship passenger with a cabin on channel side of the ship learns in Ketchikan, there are a lot of floatplanes around. It's not just flightseeing; these planes regularly ferry supplies as well as passengers to the many, many remote lodges and roadless settlements scattered throughout this part of Alaska

There are flightseeing excursions offered at all the places where your ship stops. Each area offers its own unique landscape. If you want to see glaciers and icefields, Juneau and Skagway are your best bets, but the scenery around Ketchikan and especially the Misty Fjords area is extremely dramatic. Don't be discouraged if the flightseeing excursions on your ship are sold out. Generally in each port of call, there are flightseeing trips offered by vendors on or close to the docks, so feel free to make your own arrangements. In recent years flying services delivering freight to remote communities and logging camps offered space available room for passengers as well. Such flights offer a chance to see the dramatic scenery of Southeast Alaska as well as the tiny out of the way scattered communities with only boat or plane access.

You might see some drama as well. On one recent freight flight with a few passengers aboard, the plane circled a small broken off bit of ice flow—sort of a flat iceberg—near LeConte Glacier, northeast of Petersburg. A mother seal was there with her two very cute and recently calved pups. As the plane circled and passengers and pilot looked on in horror, an orca (killer whale) zoomed out of the water, sliding across the ice, jaws snapping and leaving only bloody pieces of seal behind him as he slid into the water on the other side.

"That's not something you see every day..." said the pilot.

The ironic thing about this coast is this: all that gorgeous waterfront land.. and (hardly) any that you can buy! Basically most of the land is owned by the State of Alaska or Federal Government.

But for entrepreneurial Alaskans like this couple, that wasn't a problem. They found a sheltered cove that they liked - near a logging camp where there was a school for their children and possible work as well.

In those days the big plywood mill at Sitka and the pulp mill in Ketchikan were going full blast so there was steady traffic of floating log rafts going up and down Clarence Strait, a main north-south route. On occasion the rafts would break up in a storm or a bundle of logs would escape in rough weather. The result was that the shores were littered in places with big spruce, cedar and hemlock logs. So, after getting a permit from the Forest Service to get the logs, this couple started pulling the logs off the beach - a big job in itself - these logs are typically sixty feet long, three or four feet in diameter, and weigh several tons.

Then they assembled the logs into a raft and built a small platform to support a portable sawmill to start sawing the logs in to planks. They planked over the whole raft - another big job as you can see how big the raft is - and started building their house!

Top: It's a rare house or settlement along the winding waterways of the Inside Passage. Bottom: New floating cabin under construction, SE Alaska, 1982. While they build their larger home the family with two growing sons lives in the small cabin on the left. Opposite top: Cabin's finished, family is all in! Note the traditional native canoe tied to the really big log. The lady of the family was a Haida native and wanted to share her heritage with her children, so they all built it.

Build your house on the water!

Now living in a floating home has a few differences from living in a regular home. For instance, while this family was building the big house, they lived in the very small one on the left. And with two young rambunctious boys, sometimes on rainy days, the mom, needing a little quiet time for herself, would send the boys out to fish, in the outhouse!

Another time, the father noticed that one of his propane tanks was leaking from a cracked valve. Unable to stop the leak and worried that the fire in his fish smoker might ignite the gas, he disconnected the tank and pushed it into the water, letting it drift away with the tidal current. When it was a safe distance away, he took out his rifle, planning to put a couple of holes into the tank to sink it. Usually a crack shot, his aim was a little off that day, and instead of sinking it, the bullet knocked the valve off the end of the tank, and the jet of escaping propane send the tank shooting across the cove. And back towards the floating home where his family watched in amazement and growing horror as the speeding tank, curved around - and headed right back toward them!

Plus, each time the father got a bead on the tank with the rifle again, it would zig or zag or dive underwater like a torpedo and the bullet would miss! Finally, when it was only about 75 feet away and headed right for them, he got a good bead, and blew a hole in the end, sinking it.. Not a problem that you'd have with a house on the land...

And if you find some land... just drag that house ashore!!!

103

The landscape here is a tangle of islands, channels, harbors, and bays, usually backed up by mountains rising to snow. This is looking east from near Point Baker, Mile 742. The Canadian border runs along the highest peaks on the horizon, here the Alaska mainland is barely 30 miles wide, but the islands Stretch far to the west. Below: A fisherman's shed in the remote community of Point Baker. Away from the busy towns, where the cruise ships stop is a slower, older Alaska.

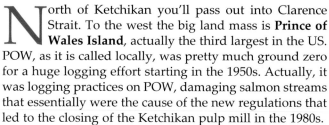

North of Ketchikan you'll pass out into Clarence Strait. To the west the big land mass is **Prince of Wales Island**, actually the third largest in the US. POW, as it is called locally, was pretty much ground zero for a huge logging effort starting in the 1950s. Actually, it was logging practices on POW, damaging salmon streams that essentially were the cause of the new regulations that led to the closing of the Ketchikan pulp mill in the 1980s.

Today, some logging still continues, but to a much lesser degree with some of the logs being shipped to Puget Sound, and others to small local sawmills.

In a sense Prince of Wales is making the transition to the new Alaska economy—more based on recreation than commercial fishing and logging. 25 years ago Craig, on the west coast of the island, was a rough Native town where commercial fishing was pretty much the main economic activity. Today Craig features a number of sportfishing lodges and has a surprising amount of second home construction. Much of this has been spurred by the paving of old logging roads and daily ferry service from Ketchikan to Hollis, on the east coast of Prince of Wales Island.

If you see some small fishing skiffs around **Mile 686**, they'll be from **Meyers Chuck,** one of a handful of roadless fishing communities scattered throughout the region. In the late 1930s, the crew of the *Maggie Murphy* stopped here, still looking for the fishing bonanza they had come so far for:

"We found a feud raging in the harbor that was as ancient and fierce as that waged between picnickers and ants. The most tedious chore the cabin dweller knows is keeping up a supply of firewood. In Alaska, stoves burn continuously for nine months of the year,

and they consume prodigious amounts of fuel. All this fuel must be obtained by felling trees and chopping them into cordwood.

"Where fishermen are living on boats, the problem is even more acute. While most boats have oil stoves, many still have old fashioned wood burners, and the owners must make frequent trips ashore in search of fuel. In Meyers Chuck, the fishermen who lived in boats piled their stove wood on the float alongside the point where they habitually docked at night.

"Once Ed and I watched a fisherman creep out of his boat and approach a nearby woodpile. He gazed furtively about to see if anyone was watching, then lifted the canvas, deftly grabbed a slab of wood, and dashed back to his boat. A few minutes later we heard him chopping, and it wasn't long before clouds of smoke were bellowing from his stove pipe.

"When the owner of the firewood came to dock, he took inventory of his woodpile and promptly missed one piece.

"Gathering firewood is the god-awfulest job in this country!" he roared, "A man that'll steal it ought to be strung up like a cattle rustler.'"

—John Joseph Ryan, *The Maggie Murphy*

With no road connection between most towns, tugs and barges are an essential part of transportation here. Note the modular homes as well as boats - pretty much everything travels by barge here! Below: Deadheads: half-sunk logs, weighing several tons and sometimes extending only a few inches above the surface, are a constant treat to boaters here. Because of them, prudent mariners are very reluctant to travel after dark in small craft.

WHERE THERE ARE NO PHONES

While the roads were being paved on Prince of Wales, one of the flaggers was Ethel Hamar, who at the time lived on a floating home–on a log raft–in Coffman Cove. One of her sons worked at a log sorting yard at Craig, on the other side of the island. With no phone connection, and not having a vehicle - Ethel took a skiff ashore and walked to work - she missed keeping up with the progress of her grandchildren in Craig. Finally her son found a novel way to communicate.

Every now and then one of the big logging trucks carrying logs from the sorting yard at Craig to a log dump on Clarence Strait would honk and slow down as it passed Ethel and call down: "Got a message from yer boy, Ethel."

On the side of one of the big logs in big spray painted red letters would be a message like: "HEY MOM, WE'RE OK, BILLY GOT HIS FIRST TOOTH THIS WEEK"

In 1982 and 1982, my wife and I had a job running a tender or fish buying vessel for the Icicle Seafoods cannery in Petersburg, between Ketchikan and Juneau. Each Sunday we'd leave Petersburg full of fuel, water, and ice and groceries for 'our fishermen' - a fleet of a dozen 30-40' salmon gillnet boats operating in a remote area of Alaska near the Canadian Border. There for the four day fishing period, we'd travel around the area, buying fish, delivering groceries, selling fuel, etc. Then late on Thursday afternoon we'd finish up buying fish, get our fishermen's 'town lists' and start steaming for Petersburg, 20 hours away.

A hard, hard way to make a buck!

One of the smaller, but most successful boats was operated by a family with two boys on board, Mike, the younger, and Stormy, the oldest. We became good friends with the whole family and I asked the mom how Stormy got his name.

"We were beach logging the winter Stormy was born. We were living in the boat then, we didn't have a house anywhere; times were tight. It was a hard way to make a winter's paycheck, but it was all we had then. Here's how it works: you lease a section of beach from the Forest Service and you get all the logs on that beach - mostly ones that had drifted ashore from log rafts that had broken up over the years. So one by one you get the logs off and make up your own log raft in a nearby sheltered cove, and then when youre all done, you have to call a tug to come and tow the logs into the sawmill in town. But you dont get paid until the logs get delivered.

"It was the hardest beach to get logs off of that I ever saw, and I was pregnant and almost due when we were finishing up. And I'd have to carry that heavy chain saw and a hydraulic jack all that way to get to those logs. It was hard.

"It was blowing when I went into labor, no time to take our boat all the way across to town, so we had to call a plane. The tug was already coming to take our logs to the pulpmill in Ketchikan, and George had to stay to help hook up the raft. He said he'd meet me in town.

"It was so gusty that floatplane had to make three tries before he could finally set down. Then I got to the hospital and you could hear the rain slashing at the windows and roaring through the trees all night long.

"But I had my baby OK - he was a healthy little boy - around 10 in the morning, and I was just laying there nursing him when George came in.

"Right away I could tell something bad had happened - I could just tell by his face.

" 'We lost them logs.' he told me right off, 'the raft broke up, coming across. The logs are all scattered. They're gone. We'll never get paid.'"

"I just lay there a moment, then said, 'Here, don't you want to hold our baby?'"

"So George picked him up and asked me what I wanted to name him.

"I thought on it for a while, and finally came up with something:

"Let's name him Stormy, for the night he was born.."

Stormy

Snow Pass: look for whales!

— Passenger Tip —

Northbound travelers: don't miss Snow Pass, about two hours or so after leaving Ketchikan.

Below: Put your binoculars on the buoy on the east side of the channel. Often there will be sea lions on it!

At **Mile 720,** about three hours after leaving Ketchikan, your ship will transit narrow **Snow Passage.** The constricted channel often creates tide rips that will bunch herring together and often attract humpback whales. Get your binoculars and go out on deck, preferably up near the bow where you can see both sides of the channel. Most ships carry a naturalist and in addition most captains are alerted to the possibility of whales here, so the presence of whales is likely to be announced. Different ships have different protocols. If there are passenger activities, and there's just a single whale blowing occasionally, it might not be announced.

If you're really fortunate and have strong binoculars, you may be able to observe bubble net feeding, a method used by humpback whales to herd fish into compact, easy-to-eat schools. The whales circle beneath the herring, exhaling slowly. The circle of bubbles serves to contain or herd the fish, and the humpbacks then surface in the middle, with their mouths open.

This area is also open to salmon gillnetting, usually fishing Sunday - Wednesday. If the fish are running the gillnetters will often work the shore near Pt. Macnamara, five miles north of the pass, off the east or right side of the ship if you are traveling northbound. The trick at this spot is get close to the beach. If there are boats there, use your binoculars; you'll be surprised how close they get.

Mural on Wrangell store wall. John Muir passed through here in 1879 and called it "a lawless draggle of wooded huts and houses." Today's visitors will find it to be a welcome change from the crowds of the main cruise ports when the big ships are in town. Below: end of an era - the last big logging truck in Wrangell is ready to be loaded onto a barge.

Off the beaten path, about 25 miles southwest of Petersburg, Wrangell's history stems from its position at the mouth of the Stikine River.

This small town was the busiest spot in Alaska when the hordes bound for the Stikine and Cassiar gold rushes poured through in 1861 and 1873, bound up the Stikine, the natural route into the interior. But when the rushes were over, Wrangell settled back down into a small fishing and logging community, with many Chinese coming to work in the canneries and the first sawmill constructed in 1888.

Compared to the bigger towns where crowds overflow the sidewalks when the big ships are in, visitors here find a welcome slower pace, perhaps encountering schoolchildren selling garnets they've dug from the riverbank, and small locally owned shops instead of the big chains.

But it is still the river that is the biggest draw. It is on the main migratory route north for many species. April is especially dramatic, when 1500 plus bald eagles congregate to feed on the hooligan (a small oily fish) run, and 8-10,000 snow geese pass through on their way north. The 160 miles between Wrangell and Telegraph Creek, in Canada, are especially dramatic, and raft or floatplane or jetboats are a great way to explore. Another visitor option is a boat trip to the Anan Creek Bear Observatory, about 30 miles south. When the fish are running, the bear are waiting for them and it's an impressive sight. Short on time? Consider a floatplane trip over Petersburg, Wrangell narrows, and LeConte Glacier.

Top: downtown: no chain jewelry or clothing stores here, this is an authentic town. Above: Seafood office, Alaska style. Right: gillnetters work on their nets in Wrangell Harbor. A major seafood company recently bought the fish plant in town, making life easier for local fishermen

Wrangell was hit especially hard when the Alaska Pulp Corporation sawmill, the town's largest employer, closed in 1994. Unlike Ketchikan and Sitka, area towns that also had big mills that closed, Wrangell did not have a strong visitor and tourism industry to fall back on. So when Wrangell Seafoods failed a decade or so later, it was an especially hard blow. Fortunately, Alaska's biggest seafood company, Trident, bought the plant and made major upgrades. Around the same time the town began cleaning up the old sawmill site, purchased the largest boat lift in SE Alaska and redeveloped the site as a major boatyard. It was a big hit and the town has high hopes that over time, it will be a major part of the local economy.

Deadliest Catch in Wrangell??

Southeast Alaska also has a king crab season, albeit a short one. I found this boat unloading crab in June directly into big plastic lined cardboard boxes, rather than going into the adjacent processing plant, which struck me as odd. But then that evening, as I was getting into the Alaska Airlines 'combi' - a 737-400 fitted out with cargo hatch/pallet tracks forward and passenger cabin aft, I saw the big boxes of live king crab being loaded as well. The entire catch was being flown live to Seattle, where they would be put into a live tank in some restaurant!

Around Town:
Klondike Bikes - 907-874-2453
Sunrise Aviation - 800-874-2319
Star Cab - 907-874-3622
Alaska Charter & Travel - 888-993-2750
Fish Wrangell - 907-874-2590
Breakaway Adventures - 888-385-2488
Muskeag Meadows Golf Course - 907-874-4653
Stikine Inn - 888-874-3388
Wrangell Hostel - 907-874-3534
Sourdough Lodge - 800-874-3613
Places to eat:
For the view: Stikine Inn
Where the locals eat: Diamond C Cafe

For more: www.wrangell.com

When the big boys come through, you better move over...!

A TALE OF WRANGELL NARROWS

Once a twisting, shallow slough, Wrangell Narrows was in such a convenient place as a shortcut—saving 70 miles off the trip between Ketchikan and Juneau—that eventually the channel was dredged, widened, and marked the channel with 60 markers and buoys.

Even so, it is still a considerable challenge at night or in fog. The problem is that the region's big tides—the water level rising or falling as much as 23 feet in six hours—create very strong currents.

In the fog and in the black the prudent mariner is best served by anchoring up off the south entrance, or tieing up to the docks in Petersburg to wait better conditions. Canneries want their fish and ferries have schedules, and sometimes they meet in the middle of the narrows:

"I hate to go through them narrows in the black and the fog, but the cannery wanted the fish, so we had to go. Then right in the narrowest place, the radio blasts in my ear: 'This is the Alaska ferry *Matanuska*, southbound at marker 16. Northbound traffic please advise.' The *Matanuska*? Just a mile ahead, and him with the tide pushing him on? I called him right back, and mister, I could hear the tension in that man's voice. '*Matanuska* back. Yeah... I see you on my radar... but you'd better pull over and let us

by... it's pretty damn tight here.' We were right below Burnt Island Reef, and I could see his target on the radar getting bigger and bigger all the time. So I just slowed down and pulled over into the shallows. I'd rather put 'er ashore on a mud bank than get T-boned by a 400- foot ferry!

"I slowed right down until I was just idling into the current, and looked out into the black, trying to see him. You know how it is with that radar. When something gets really close, it just disappears into the sea clutter in the middle of the screen and you can't really tell exactly where it is. Well, the ferry did that and I was just bracing myself to hit either the shore or him, when I saw him—just a glimpse of a row of portholes rushing by fast in the night, the big tide pushing him on and then he was gone. Man, I don't know how them fellows do it, but I know I wouldn't have liked to been him that night."

—An Alaskan tender skipper

If you are on an Alaska ferry or a small cruise ship, chances are you'll travel through **Wrangell Narrows** to Petersburg. Set in one of the most dramatic landscapes in the region with 10,000' Kates Needle rising spectacularly behind, the town is known as Little Norway for its original descendants, who settled here after coming from the old country.

With strong shrimp, salmon, crab, and halibut resources close at hand and icebergs very conveniently drifting right into the boat harbor from nearby Le Conte Glacier, it was a commercial fisherman's dream: before the advent of refrigeration, locals would ice their fish with iceberg ice and ship them south to Seattle markets. Eventually, three salmon canneries, a shrimp processor, and a cold storage plant served the needs of its fishermen.

I first skippered a 'big boat' here - a 60' fish buyer or tender. My boss, John Enge, grew up in Petersburg. Before he started school, he only spoke Norwegian, learned at home, and Tlingit, learned from his native playmates.

Until about 1985, the Petersburg fishermen mostly worked the waters of Southeast Alaska. With markets for Alaska seafood expanding with the robust Japanese economy, Petersburg fishermen and a locally owned cannery, Icicle Seafoods, made a major expansion into fisheries in

the remote areas of western Alaska, particularly the Bering Sea and Bristol Bay.

When many seafood markets weakened in the 1990s with the major slump in the Japanese economy, Petersburg fishing companies were mostly able to survive, while some others in Wrangell, Ketchikan, and Juneau had to close their doors.

Compared to British Columbia, the salmon stocks of Alaska have proved remarkably resilient over the years. 2011 was a particularly good year - a number of seiners had caught a million pounds which pencils out to a $55,000 crew share each for a summer's work and the word on the street was that there was at least one boat that had caught two million. A number of men have careers and families in other parts of the country, only to return to Petersburg each summer to get in on the commercial harvest.

Today, while tourism plays a huge part in the economy of most towns in the region, here it is conspicuously absent. The harbor isn't large enough for the big ships, and candidly, the town fathers prefer to concentrate on what they know best: fishing. Nevertheless, small cruise ships—100 passengers and less—often stop here, as does the Alaska ferry.

It's not all just commercial fishing - Petersburg is both the jumping off place for several remote lodges, as well

Top: Locals relax next to a small iceberg while they pick the tails of the harvest of their shrimp pot and below, cooking a few up for the way home!

Opposite top: Seiners tied up in downtown Petersburg. Opposite bottom: Norwegian pride: a worker in the egg room sports his favorite hat!

Ky Michael Thomassen
"Fishing is not a matter
of life or death, it is
more serious than that."

Ole Sjonning Husvik
1890 - 1961
"Ya, vi ha it god in America"

Steven D. Bergman
1959 - 1993
My glory was
I had such friends.

as remote cabins that you can rent through the US Forest Service: www.fs.fed.us/r10/tongass/cabins/cabins.shtml

If you do visit, stop by the harbormaster's office, just off main street, with canneries on either side. There you can pick up a town map, etc.

Two big events are the **Little Norway Festival** celebrating Norwegian Independence Day in mid May, where traditional costumes and crafts are in evidence, and Fourth of July, a bit more raucous, as the fishing fleet is usually in town.

Hammer Slough is close by with the **Sons of Norway Hall** and **Sing Yee Alley,** an excellent place for local crafts, and the **Clausen Museum** celebrating local commercial fishing.

A nice stroll is just along the waterfront, north out of town. On the right you'll see the homes fishermen and processors built overlooking Frederick Sound and the entrance to Wrangell Narrows. From their view homes it was a short walk down to either the boat harbor or 'cannery row.' Not a bad life.

Top: net sheds in Hamar Slough - at high tide boats could tie up at the sheds and receive or unload gear. Above: Navigation marker in Wrangell Narrows in front of town - at high tide the water level is right up to the very top. In the distance are Kate's Needle (10,049') and Devil's Thumb (9.077') Opposite page: cannery row with high mountains behind - you can see Norwegian immigrants might have felt at home here. Cans being readied to be filled with salmon, and memorial plaques.

117

In earlier days, Alaska cruises were more casual. In addition to passengers, the ships often carried freight bound to remote canneries and villages up and down the coast. These stops usually only took an hour or so, and passengers usually didn't leave the ship, but still, they got a slice of life today's cruise ship passengers are unlikely to see. Photos courtesy F. Garland Swain. Top: the big stamp mill at Juneau, above the present cruise docks. Opposite top: Saxman Village. S.S. Jefferson brochure at right from author's collection.

Alaska Cruise,
S.S. Alaska
Circa 1950

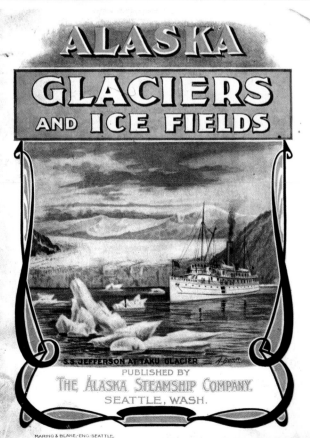

ALASKA GLACIERS AND ICE FIELDS

S.S. JEFFERSON AT TAKU GLACIER

PUBLISHED BY
THE ALASKA STEAMSHIP COMPANY,
SEATTLE, WASH.

MARING & BLAKE.-ENG.-SEATTLE.

SS. ALASKA

Turbo-Electric Drive—Twin Screw

Length	366 feet
Breadth	49 feet
Displacement	7,450 tons
Gross	4,658 tons
Maximum capacity	220 first class passengers

During the 1950 summer season SS. ALASKA is scheduled to sail from Seattle on alternate Thursdays, as shown in complete schedule in this folder. Ports of call are:

NORTHBOUND: Ketchikan, Petersburg, Juneau, Seward.

SOUTHBOUND: Valdez, Cordova, Juneau, Petersburg, Ketchikan, Seattle.

SS. ALASKA is scheduled to remain a minimum of three hours at Juneau, Valdez and Cordova, and to arrive in Seward early Tuesday morning for connection with train to Anchorage. Ship is scheduled to depart Seward southbound at 9:00 p. m. Tuesdays, following arrival of boat train from Anchorage. At Valdez southbound bus passengers arriving from Fairbanks over the Richardson Highway will be embarked. As SS. ALASKA must pass through beautiful Wrangell Narrows at high tide enroute to Petersburg, on some northbound voyages call at Ketchikan may be limited to ½ hour.

SS. ALASKA has accommodations as shown below. All staterooms are first-class and all have hot and cold running water. A few staterooms are "inside" with ventilator opening to deck above. Four deluxe staterooms and six standard upper deck staterooms have two lower berths and folding upper berth. All other staterooms have two berths only. Exclusive occupancy of any stateroom requires payment of two adult fares. One-way fares are shown elsewhere in this folder. Round trip first class fares, including berth and meals, per passenger, are as follows:

Standard lower deck stateroom, no private bath, some "inside" rooms, per adult	$198.00
Standard upper deck stateroom, no private bath, per adult	219.00
Standard stateroom with private shower and toilet, upper and lower berth, can be connected with standard upper deck stateroom, per adult	263.00
Superior stateroom, private shower and toilet, single bed and folding upper berth, per adult	285.00
Deluxe stateroom, private tub and shower bath and toilet, twin beds and folding upper berth, per bed	307.00
Per upper berth in room with private bath (sold only to third person in room)	219.00
Children, ages 5 to 11 inclusive, in standard stateroom without private bath, ½ adult fare. Fares in other accommodations on request.	
Children, ages 2 to 4 inclusive	33.00
Children, under 2 years of age	no charge
15% federal tax applies on all fares.	

Top: Steamer Mariposa on the rocks in Lama Passage, BC, in 1915. MOHAI She got off, but hit the rocks for good two years later off Point Baker, on the rock that now bears her name. Below: young fisherman and friend.

Salmon gillnetters usually work the Sumner Strait area, Mile 740-745, typically fishing from Sunday noon to Thursday noon. The fish come from the west here, and the trick is to set your net back from the district boundary at Point Baker, so that the ebbing current carries you to the line, then stops, just as the tide turns. This gives you a front row seat, with no room for another boat to set legally between you and the incoming fish. There is also a nasty tide rip, nicknamed 'the big meanie,' which blasts around the corner from the west on the bigger tides, which has given an ugly surprise to many an unsuspecting gillnetter.

It was this strongly flowing tidal current that caused Captain Johnny O'Brien's luck to run out in the black of a November night in 1917. The *Mariposa* was one of the finest steamers on the Alaska run, but while Dynamite Johnny caught a nap in his stateroom as a pilot steered, the strong current set her off course and onto Mariposa Reef, **mile 745,** where parts of her still remain.

Watch for humpback whales at Point Baker, mile 745, usually in close to the shore, west of the point. Typically a pair remains here for most of the summer, feeding on herring in the tide rips. In the 1960s, a particular whale got to be known as Ma Baker. Local lore has it that she once surfaced under one of the puddle jumpers, or small fishing skiffs, lifting the surprised

fishermen and his boat completely clear of the water for a moment. Point Baker and the nearby community of Port Protection are two roadless fishing communities. It was here that we built our little island homestead in 1973.

Port Protection was the occasion of one of Vancouver's closest calls. Late on the afternoon of September 8, 1793, while exploring and charting Sumner Strait, a storm was seen approaching the area. It was at last light that Lieutenant Broughton in the *Chatham* saw the entrance to what looked like a cove and signalled Vancouver to follow him into the bay, south of **mile 745**. It was just in time:

> "We had scarcely furled the sails, when the wind shifting to the S.E., the threatened storm from that quarter began to blow, and continued with increasing violence during the whole night; we had, however, very providentially reached an anchorage that completely sheltered us from its fury, and most probably from imminent danger, if not from total destruction. Grateful for such an asylum, I named it Port Protection."
>
> —Captain George Vancouver, *A Voyage of Discovery*

To the north here are two separate major islands, Kuiu Island on the west and Kupreanof Island to the east. Between them is **Keku Strait**, known locally as **Rocky Pass**, a popular shortcut for small craft.

Top: Under the seaweed, Sumner Strait. The crab is a dungeness, target of a major fishery up and down coast from California to Alaska. M L Upton photo Below: Net colors are critical to salmon gillnetters. The net on the left is a Sumner Straits net, while the bluer one on the right is a Lynn Canal net, where the ground up dust from the many glaciers make the water a bluer color.

Above: Troller entering the very narrow entrance to Hole-in-the-Wall. It's quite an experience to pick your way in here on a day when it's stormy on the outside, and enter the unruffled lake-like basin on the inside. Top: my neighbor Alan, in his Port Protection homestead.

Hole in the Wall, east of **mile 751**, is one of Southeast Alaska's special places. From my 1973 fishing journal:

"Of all the places we visit each year, this is one of my favorites. It's like a lake in the woods, with grassy flats and steep hills above. The dusk came with muted colors, and a deer slipped out of the woods to drink in a stream. We did the dishes after supper and sat up for a bit. I don't suppose this bay sees 20 visitors a year. Within a few years the loggers will be here; they're just over the mountains now. And when they come, I don't believe I'll be back."

An hour or so past Point Baker, the vessel track turns sharply northward again at **Cape Decision Light, mile 773** and into **Chatham Strait.**

On some itineraries, like Seattle or Vancouver to Juneau, you'll come up the outside of Prince of Wales and Dall Islands. Look for dramatic **Helm Point**, at **Mile 730W**, a conspicuous headland on Coronation Island, 10 miles south. Rising sheer from the sea to a thousand feet, it is the nesting place for thousands of sea birds.

Imagine: cheap waterfront land and good fishing close at hand. This was the situation at the remote and roadless communities of Point Baker and nearby Port Protection (south of **mile 745**) in the early 1970s. A person could get an acre-sized waterfront lot on a sheltered cove, with the right to harvest a substantial amount of timber each year from the adjacent forest to use for lumber. So if you couldn't afford store-bought lumber, you could build your house from the nearby trees and make enough cash fishing salmon from an outboard skiff to support a family.

A floating store/bar/fish-buyer at Point Baker served the needs of the hundred or so souls settled around these two coves on the edge of the vast woods. The mail and freight boat came once a week, supplemented by the occasional floatplane. Families with gillnetters or trollers tried to make a trip to town—Wrangell or Petersburg, each about 40 miles away, a long day's round trip—every few months to stock up on supplies a little cheaper.

Behind the shore was the forest—thick, almost impenetrable. For the most part walking was so difficult everyone traveled by outboard. At Point

Top: Skiff fishermen at sunset, Point Baker. The fishing grounds were close enough that a person could make a living salmon fishing in small craft. Bottom: Herring for bait was abundant and could be had by just setting a small gillnet overnight.

123

Top: With dock space in town for working on nets scarce, my friends and I scavenged big float logs off the beach, ordered lumber from the sawmill in Wrangell and built our own float. Bottom: A gillnet comes in. A foot pedal controls the drum that pulls the net in. This is a 'dead man's' control; getting pulled off your feet by the net stops the drum! Right: The Point Baker floating Post Office in 1974. Mail came in once a week.

Baker, especially, one's traveling decisions were dictated by the tide. Have a whiskey warmup some snowy winter afternoon with your groceries at the store? Stay too late and the trip home might be a nightmare: wading along the shallow channel, towing your skiff behind you, lifting, scraping it over the thin places, picking your way with the flashlight through the snow, and hoping your batteries last until you make it home.

When I arrived here with my former wife on our 32-foot gillnetter in the spring of 1972, the flavor of the place was compelling. The older residents welcomed younger blood, and the salmon fishing in Sumner Strait was great. We found part of an island, on a private cove, with a gorgeous western exposure and view, for $17,000. After the season, in our houseboat on Seattle's Lake Union, we made plans for a cabin on our newly- purchased land in Point Baker. As our money dwindled, so did the size of our new-home-to-be until whatever roof we could get over our heads for fifteen hundred bucks would have to be it. We settled on a 16-by-20-foot box with a half loft, 480-square-feet, total, tiny, but it would have all that we needed.

With tight-fisted determination, we scoured garage sales and discount building suppliers. At a second-hand store we found a big diesel oil range for $35; at another, all our windows and doors for $175. In my tiny floating shop I prefabbed a Formica kitchen

At The Point Baker Floating Bar

Conveniently located on a raft of big logs, tying up at the Point Baker Bar allowed you to avoid having to make your way down a steep ramp to your boat at low tide after hoisting a few with your fishing buddies after a hard day "on the grounds."

On a busy Saturday night with all the fleet in, you'd better be wearing your boots as well, as when it got crowded, water would begin to seep through the floor as the log raft settled with the load!

Being a bit of a rough and tumble place, it offered less of a drink selection than some visitors are used to in other places. Once, a couple arrived on their nice new gillnetter, fresh in from the run up from Seattle and went in to toast the upcoming salmon season.

"What'll it be?" said the burly bartender who was also the fish buyer in town.

"What d'ya want, honey?" said the newcomer to his nicely coiffed wife.

"Hmmm," said she, "How about a Manhattan? That'd go down pretty smooth..."

"Look guys," said the bartender, "We got whiskey and water, whiskey and coke, and whiskey and tang. And we save the ice for the fish. So what'll it be?"

Top: View out our front window in 1975. If you are a commercial fisherman and can look out your front window and see your boat moored peacefully below your house, you are living your dream! Below: Fuel delivery! Romey Kaleski, a local homesteader, prepares to tow a drum of gas, delivered by a fish buying boat, back to his waterfront home. Gas is lighter than water so a drum floats!

counter top, complete with sink and drawers. We got plywood, nails, and shingles, all on deep discount, and purchased a 16-foot cedar skiff with a 10-horsepower 1958 Evinrude outboard. Tool by tool, fitting by fitting, we packed all the supplies and extras aboard my 32-foot gillnet vessel and skiff to tow north.

Shortly after arriving in Point Baker, the mail boat arrived with our pickup truck sized bundle of lumber, The plan had been to tow the tightly strapped bundle of lumber through the narrow back channel to our secluded cove and house site, but it was so green and dense, it wouldn't even float. It was what was locally called "pond dried."

So we had to set it temporarily on the dock and then haul it in our skiff, load by load, to our cove.

In the two weeks before the salmon season began we struggled: the wood was so wet it splashed when your hammer missed the nail. My one and only hand saw bent on the first beam we cut. It rained every day! Every night we would take the skiff back to our boat at the Point Baker dock, heat up something quick, and fall, exhausted, shivering, into our sleeping bags.

We created something exquisite: out of every window was the water. As we ate at the driftwood table, we could see eagles swooping low over the cove. There were curious seals, and most marvelous of all, a pair of humpbacks that hung out in the tide rips by West Rock, off the mouth of our cove. On still nights, we could hear the sigh-like breathing of the whales as they surfaced and exchanged fresh air for stale. When the first snow came one November evening, the fire in the wood stove crackled cheerily, our kerosene lamp shone out on the vast and wild world beyond the windows, and it was magic.

In summer, with daylight that lasted from four in the morning until after eleven at night, the focus was fishing: making enough to make it through the long winter. When the season was over, there was time for the kind of relaxed visiting that is a highlight of life in such places.

Seeking greener pastures, I sold my cabin at Point Baker in the mid-1980s and built a new boat for the remote salmon fishery in Bristol Bay, Alaska, 1,000 miles west. Bleak, austere, remote, with violent tidal currents and few good harbors, Bristol Bay was the opposite of Southeast Alaska. The fishing was a competitive frenzy I'd never experienced before, but many of my friends from Point Baker and Southeast Alaska were there and the shorter season allowed us more time at home with our families and children.

Yet to a man (Alaska law allows salmon fishermen to fish only a single region), we all missed the wooded waterways and secluded harbors we'd left behind.

Working on your net is an integral part of salmon fishing! Below: A salmon fishing family enjoys a little free time between the weekly fishing periods.

127

Old Flea was pretty much a fixture around Point Baker in the 1970s. "Been a baseball player, down south.." one story had it, "Was a handlogger back in the day.." another said. All I really knew that he was a salmon hand troller at Point Baker as long as anyone could remember, fishing out of an open skiff and that he lived in a tiny cabin on the back channel, that he was a regular at our little floating bar.

A lot of young folks were coming to Point Baker and nearby Port Protection in those days. Hand trolling was an inexpensive way to enter the fishery. The newcomers were mostly a longhaired bunch, shunned by the older more conservative fishermen in the community. But not Flea. He welcomed the new blood, became sort of The Patriarch of the hand troll fleet.

And was so generous. He had his monthly Social Security check, his cabin was all paid for. Each summer, it would seem that one of the young couples that came to Baker to fish were down on their luck. It was Flea that would take them in, take them fishing each day, show them the best places, how to rig the gear. And until they got on their feet, he'd give them his fish money.

Above is my favorite picture of him. Just finished selling his fish for the day - at Point Baker, the fish buyer was also the bartender - and headed home, beer in hand. Not a bad retirement at all...

CELEBRATION 2010

Sponsored by the Sealaska Heritage Institute, Celebration is a bi-annual Alaska Native festival showcasing the traditions of the Haida, Tlingit, and Tsimshian cultures. These photos were taken in June of 2010, during the parade at the end of Celebration.

4TH GEN. TSIMPSHEAN DANCERS
METLAKATLA

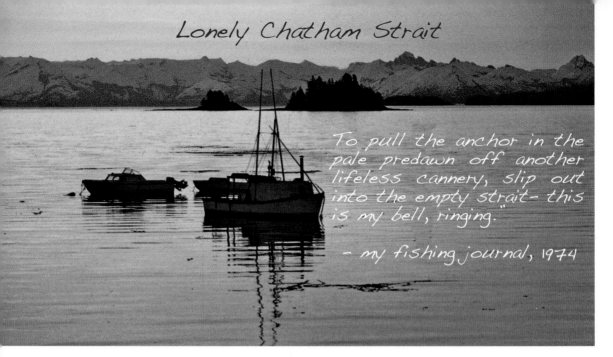

"To pull the anchor in the pale predawn off another lifeless cannery, slip out into the empty strait - this is my bell, ringing."

— my fishing journal, 1974

Baranof Island looms at dawn, looking west from the native village of Kake. Below: An old timer at Port Alexander remembers the old days when hand trollers set up their tents all around the harbor to fish the run of big king and sliver salmon running at Cape Ommaney.

For much of this century, **Chatham Strait** was a beehive of activity. Between the salmon plants, the herring plants, and the whaling stations, almost every bay in this canyon-like region was home to some sort of commercial activity, frenzied during the summer fishing season, and sleepier in winter, with usually just a caretaker and his family keeping a watch on things. Then the herring and the whales disappeared, and refrigerated tenders allowed consolidation of the salmon canneries into towns like Petersburg and Ketchikan.

For the small craft traveler today, it is almost spooky to travel in Chatham Strait, to anchor and go ashore and wander in the ruins, rarely encountering another traveler.

One of the few settlements along here is **Port Alexander, Mile 792.** With a good harbor, a settlement, a fish buyer and a store, and good fishing at Cape Ommaney (west of mile 786), it's a popular spot in summer. In its heyday, the 1920s and 1930s, it was Alaska with a capital A, as the *Maggie Murphy* boys noted:

> "It became the number one trolling port in the territory, a wide-open, carefree, money-kissed little place that old-timers still recall with nostalgia."
> —John Joseph Ryan, *The Maggie Murphy*

When they walked into town, they were halted by an elderly man who told them, "Boys, it's illegal to

THAN OF THE DEEP
WHALE 65 FEET LONG

walk on the streets of Port Alexander sober."

In those days, many trollers worked out of open boats, some without motors, rowing as they towed their lines through the water. A little tent city sprang up south of the dock each summer. By the late 1940s the party was over. The great runs rapidly diminished as the newly-built dams on the Columbia River, 1,200 miles south, prevented the big kings from reaching their spawning grounds.

At **Port Conclusion**, three miles north of Port Alexander, Vancouver anxiously awaited the four overdue cutters and yawl boats that were filling in the last blank places on his chart in August, 1794. Finally the boats hove safely into sight during a rainstorm on the 19th.

Then with grog for all hands, and cheers ringing from ship to ship in a remote cove halfway around the world from England, there ended one of the most remarkable feats of navigation and exploration in modern times. In three summers of exploring and charting this unknown coast, through persistent fogs, swift currents and occasional thick ice— losing

Top: sperm whale at the Port Armstrong whaling station, around 1910. MOHAI 15329 Below: the old general store at Killisnoo.. Today the Whaler's Cove Lodge is located near here.

No one knows why humpback whales breach, but they seem to like to do it a lot in Stephens Passage. Photograph by Duncan Kowalski.

just one man to bad shellfish— Vancouver had disproved the ages-old notion of a Northwest Passage back to the Atlantic. In doing so, he charted, explored, described and named much of the Northwest coast. It was nothing less than a stunning achievement. He was 38 years old.

The village visible to the southeast from **mile 845** is **Kake**, a Tlingit village supported by a cannery and logging on native land. Locals use narrow Rocky Pass frequently as a short cut to Sumner Strait. According to one story they were astounded a few years back, to see a tug towing a big barge emerging from the constricted passage. No one could remember such a big vessel or barge coming through the pass before. The skipper stepped out and hailed some locals fishing from a skiff:

"Say," the rough-looking man said, waving a hand back toward Rocky Pass, "that Wrangell Narrows ain't nothing like the chart." He stopped and looked over at the village on the shore, "And I thought Petersburg was larger than this." He was 40 miles west of where he thought he was!

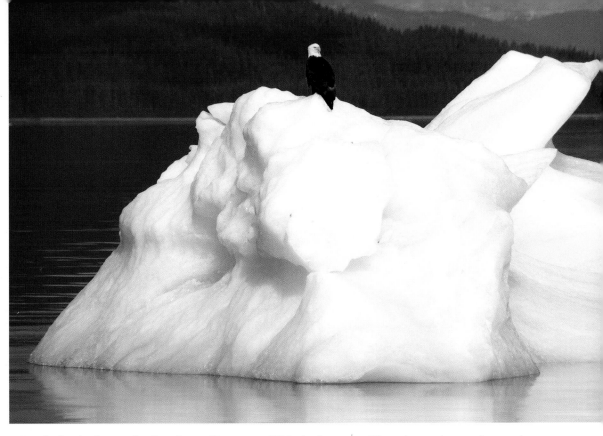

Look for icebergs in Stephens Passage. This is the southern limit of drift ice from the glaciers in Tracy and Endicott Arms, east of **Mile 900**, and Le Conte Glacier, east of Petersburg. In the 70s and 80s when I was running fishing buying boats and gillnetting in this area, ice was a big hazard.

It doesn't take much of an iceberg to puncture the hull of a fiberglass or wooden fishing boat. Plus ice is not very buoyant so an iceberg the size of a dump truck would hardly show above the surface of the water, and be almost impossible to see on radar if there was any kind of a choppy sea running or a swell driving up from the Gulf of Alaska. So boats would travel very cautiously in these waters if visibility was poor.

The icebergs did have benefits though. When I was a fish buyer, trying to save time and fuel on the long run up to Chilkat Inlet in Lynn Canal, **Mile 1000N**, we'd pull up as close as we could to the biggest iceberg we could find - tie right to it if it was calm - and turn on our pumps and suck the cold water right around the iceberg into our big insulated fish hold and thus save hours of running the noisy refrigeration system!

There is a major sea lion rookery on the mainland shore east of **Mile 890**. Sea Lions are common throughout the area where you will be cruising and can often be seen sleeping on buoys.

What happened
to all
these places?

On a wonderfully fair summer evening, back in fish buying days in the 70s, we dropped the anchor in the protected anchorage at Cape Fanshaw, about 100 miles south of Juneau. Launched the skiff, motored in to the beach to walk around this exquisite abandoned homestead. An orchard's apples ripened on the trees, deer tracks evident in the soft ground. We explored in awe, marveling at the site: a protected anchorage, southwest exposure, gardens gone wild, obvious products of a fertile soil.

The original owners were gone. Someone, probably a traveling skiff fisherman, had squatted for a while, maybe even the summer before, judging by the recent plastic in the windows. Near the beach was an old boiler, on the shore, pillings. Clearly there had been more than a homestead here; perhaps in earlier days there had been a fish processing plant as well. But then, except for some cans the squatter had left, there was no sign of recent habitation.

35 years later I came again, this time with a friend, to video some of what was there and what I had felt. Before we came around the point, I was thinking that maybe there was a lodge there now, that it was probably private land, and that surely someone would have taken advantage of such a promising spot.

We found the trees tall and dark, the settlement, the homestead that seemed just to wait for settlers in 1975, gone. Only by exploring the thick underbrush did we find the old house: the trees pushing up through it.

Why? I wondered. I'd seen it before - a fox farm on Harbor Island, and abandoned settlements up and down the Inside Passage, only flowering shrubs in the spring or bright deciduous trees in the fall, standing out sharply in the endless miles of evergreens along the shore to reveal them.

Years before, I'd rooted among the drawers in the old superintendent's office in the now abandoned big cannery at Butedale, B.C. It was a Royal Canadian Mounted Police report of an old settler, found shot by his own hand, in a remote homestead that gave me a clue. There was no note; but the circumstances made the reasons plain: loneliness and failing health.

These little places needed a critical mass of settlers, it seemed to me. Without it, the dark long winters were simply too much.

Cape Fanshaw, 1975

Cape Fanshaw, 2009

Tracy Arm, 1972. Don't let your dog off on an iceberg; they don't like it... Below: If you look carefully at the walls, you can see the striations—long gouges or scratches made by the glacier as it moved down the canyon.

Many ships enter Tracy Arm around 6 a.m. so they can get to Juneau for a port call in time for passengers to go on their shore excursions

If yours does: get up early! The entrance, particularly that first right angle turn is truly spectacular, as the light can be exquisite at that time of day.

Traveling up Tracy Arm (the entrance is five miles northeast of **Mile 900**) is like going back through geologic history. The fjord's dramatic walls lose their vegetation until they become bare shining rock, shaped and ground smooth by the ice. In many places the mountains plunge vertically into the water, which is more than a thousand feet deep.

Muir was genuinely moved by the power and the beauty of the glaciers, and he was able to communicate some of this enthusiasm to his companions. Once, when they had paddled most of an afternoon up Tracy Arm, frustrated with the narrow and ice-choked channel, they turned yet another corner and found what he had come to seek, the glacier itself. While Muir stood in the canoe, sketching the glacier, several huge icebergs calved off, thundering into the water of the narrow fjord. "The ice mountain is well disposed toward you," one of the native paddlers said to Muir. "He is firing his big guns to welcome you."

Tracy Arm Tip:

Get Up Early!

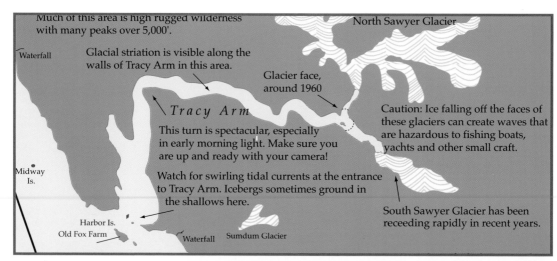

Much of this area is high rugged wilderness with many peaks over 5,000'.

North Sawyer Glacier

Waterfall

Glacial striation is visible along the walls of Tracy Arm in this area.

Glacier face, around 1960

Tracy Arm

This turn is spectacular, especially in early morning light. Make sure you are up and ready with your camera!

Caution: Ice falling off the faces of these glaciers can create waves that are hazardous to fishing boats, yachts and other small craft.

Midway Is.

Watch for swirling tidal currents at the entrance to Tracy Arm. Icebergs sometimes ground in the shallows here.

South Sawyer Glacier has been receeding rapidly in recent years.

Harbor Is.
Old Fox Farm

Waterfall   Sumdum Glacier

Right: Entering Tracy Arm aboard the 110 passenger ship, Spirit of Oceanus. Be sure to set your alarm and get up early—the entrance is a dramatic twisting canyon.

Tracy is especially suited for small ships, that can get up close to the ice. Many, like the Spirit of Oceanus group here, use inflatable boats or Zodiacs to explore the shore. The area close to the glacier is narrow and can be congested with ice; large ships might not be able to get as close to the ice as their passengers might like. Occasionally there is too much ice or the fog is too thick for good ice viewing, so Captains of large ships might choose an alternate destination, almost equally as dramatic: Endicott Arm, See Pages 148-149

The adventure started in Juneau when pilot Jacques picked me up. Turns out Jacques had also put in his time as a fish buyer so we had plenty to talk about. Top: small grounded iceberg, Fords Terror. Right: stunning and magical to behold and approach, this is the iceberg that almost finished your author!

I was mighty glad to see my buddy, Dan's, boat when pilot Jacques banked in over Harbor Island, at the entrance to Tracy Arm, 90 miles south of Juneau. I hadn't spoken to Dan for a week; he was bringing his fishing boat up from Petersburg and out of cell phone range. If he wasn't at the rendezvous, I didn't have plan B.

Jacques slid in for smooth landing and Dan and I were off for a photo session in the dramatic fjord called Fords Terror, a few hours south.

Now Dan and I are very experienced - between us we have 50 plus years of experience on Alaskan waters. We know how careful you have to be around icebergs, how their center of gravity changes as they melt, how they can capsize without warning...

So at the entrance to Ford's Terror and was this totally spectacular iceberg, maybe 200 feet long with a graceful arch perhaps 40 feet high, the biggest one I had ever seen: stunning. We assumed, from its position near the entrance to the narrow inner basin that it was grounded: sitting on the bottom, and therefore stable.

Jumping in the small outboard powered inflatable skiff with our cameras, we circled that gorgeous iceberg in awe, stopped the engine and drifted, close to the arch, but not underneath. It was a Zen-like experience: we could feel the ice's cold breath on our faces, hear the slow hiss of bubbles rising from its submerged mass beneath us. The blue translucent arch just tow-

The BAD Iceberg
at Ford's Terror

ered over us, seemingly lit from within. The sea was still, in the distance was the whisper of a waterfall tumbling down the canyon wall: it was magic.

Then there was this rumble that we felt through the water more than heard. Dan turned to me with a smile, "The iceberg is talking to us."

Just then the iceberg broke in half at the top of the arch, almost directly over our heads. Our cameras both hanging from our necks, stunned into inaction, we gaped as the nearer half toppled toward us, as if in slow motion, smacking into the water a few feet behind our outboard motor. Only when the other half toppled away from us, and the previously underwater part started to emerge from the water, pushing our inflatable back, rolling water into the boat, did we have the presence of mind to start the motor and dart away, lest an emerging ice projection catch our skiff and flip it.

"OK," we reassured ourselves afterwards, "what was the worst that could have happened? We'd be in the water, our cameras would be ruined, but we could have flipped the skiff back over, and paddled back (a half mile) to the *Sue Anne* and warmed up..."

Or not...

So.. take it from a couple of really experienced guys: don't get close to icebergs if you are in small craft!

"Sept 5, 1973: Just at one, traveling dead slow, with little water under us, we passed the rapids in the creek-like entrance to Fords Terror. Hardly spoke a word for the next mile, so overpowering was the scenery. The sun went over the mountain at 4:30, and the evening came early and chill. At dusk, flight after flight of ducks came in low and fast, to settle on the water near the shore with a rush of many wings and soft callings.

"The night was chilly, with northern lights again. Stood out on deck and watched, until the cold drove us in. Yesterday and today, the places we visited make us feel tiny indeed.

"September 6, 1973: First frost! The stove went out in the night, and we woke to find the dog nestled in between us. To go out onto the frosty deck on such a morning, with the still glassy basin around, and the dark forests and frozen hills above— words can't tell it, pictures can't show it.

"Our cup seems pretty full just now."

- from my journal

Top: Our salmon boat inside Fords Terror, 1972. In those days it was little visited. Today, fly-in kayak groups and intrepid boaters occasionally visit. Above: June, 2010: Ice scoured vertical wall inside Fords Terror reveals its glacial origin.

147

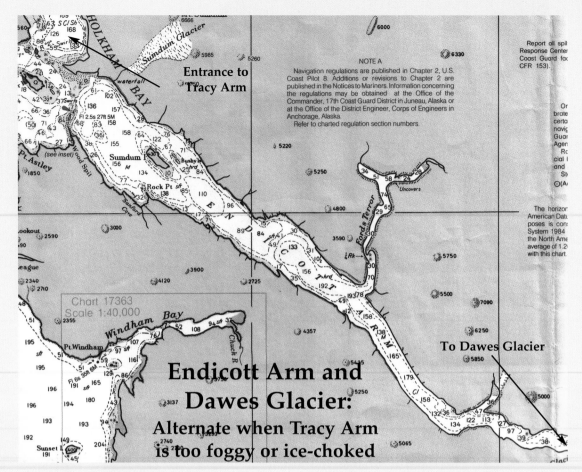

NOTE A

Navigation regulations are published in Chapter 2, U.S. Coast Pilot 8. Additions or revisions to Chapter 2 are published in the Notices to Mariners. Information concerning the regulations may be obtained at the Office of the Commander, 17th Coast Guard District in Juneau, Alaska or at the Office of the District Engineer, Corps of Engineers in Anchorage, Alaska.

Refer to charted regulation section numbers.

Entrance to Tracy Arm

To Dawes Glacier

Chart 17363
Scale 1:40,000

Endicott Arm and Dawes Glacier:
Alternate when Tracy Arm is too foggy or ice-choked

John Muir explored this area in 1880. From his journal:

"During the night I was awakened by the beating of the spent ends of berg-waves against the side of my tent, though I had fancied myself well beyond their reach. These special waves are not raised by wind or tide, but by the fall of large bergs from the snout of the glacier, or sometimes by the overturning or breaking of large bergs that may have long floated in perfect poise. The highest berg-waves oftentimes travel half a dozen miles or farther before they are much spent, producing a singularly impressive uproar in the far recesses of the mountains on calm dark nights when all beside is still. Far and near they tell the news that a berg is born, repeating their story again and again, compelling attention and reminding us of earth-quake-waves that roll on for thousands of miles, taking their story from continent to continent."

149

Top: a whale watching excursion.
Below: native dancer with traditional
button robe.

A bear? Behind the espresso stand? No roads in or out? You have to come by boat or plane? What kind of a state capital is this? Probably different from what you're used to...

Almost surrounded by high mountains and with a vast ice field—larger than Rhode Island—to the north, Juneau winters are substantially colder than Ketchikan or Sitka. Tlingit natives had fish camps near today's downtown, but wintered in a more temperate and sheltered area near Auke Bay.

In 1880, Kowee, the local Tlingit chief, led two prospectors, Joe Juneau and Richard Harris, up Gold Creek, which runs through today's downtown, to what is now Silver Bow Basin. The men found ample nuggets and quartz laced with gold, and Alaska's first gold rush was on.

However, the easy to find streambed gold was quickly gathered up, and a new kind of enterprise was formed to follow the gold underground. This industrial scale deep tunnel hard rock mining was very different from other Alaska gold rushes where individuals or small groups of men worked creeks and beaches with essentially hand tools.

At Juneau, high grade ore was quickly exhausted and

Juneau Area

Top: cabin on the road headed out to the Last Chance Basin - this is literally about 5 blocks from downtown. Below: sculptures made from sperm whale teeth in a downtown gallery. Opposite top: view from a Princess ship as it leaves town. Opposite lower: 5 turbo DeHavilland Otters waiting for excursion passengers in front of the Hangar Bar, a fun eatery. Residents like these planes much better than the old Beavers which were very loud.

massive stamp mills were built to extract gold; it wasn't uncommon for 20 or more tons of ore to be dug and processed to yield a single ounce of fine gold. The tailings—the crushed rock that was left, was dumped along the shore, creating the flat land on which today's downtown Juneau was built. At peak capacity, the big stamp mills of the Alaska-Juneau mine, still visible above the cruise ship docks, could crush 12,000 tons of ore a day. Working conditions were dangerous! The entrance to the big Treadwell mine was nicknamed the "glory Hole," for all the miners—sometimes one a week—that went to glory there. Eventually the gold played out, the tunnels— by then deep under the channel—filled with water, and today all that's left is ruins of the old stamp mill on the hill above the cruise ship dock.

But the gold is still there and a 21st century style mine— designed with minimal visual and environmental impact—is being built on a slope above Lynn Canal, 45 miles north of Juneau.

The gold made Juneau the economic capital, so the legislative capital was moved there as well from Sitka in 1906. As the gold played out, government jobs, both state and federal, assumed a dominant role in Juneau's economy.

Because of these government jobs, economic life in Juneau is much less seasonal than in other Alaska coastal towns which are more dependent on tourism and sport and commercial fishing. For this reason, the impact of the growing cruise ship industry sets a little less easy with Juneau residents. Cruise ship captains have learned that if they want to avoid an angry call from the harbormaster, they need to keep their deck public address systems off as they pass Douglas (across the channel from Juneau) as they approach and leave town. Another source of annoyance to locals is the noise created by the flightseeing helicopters and float planes, which echo up off the steep rock walls behind town. In order to avoid the air pollution that occurs when four or five big thousand footers are running their generators in the harbor, cruise operators have installed dock wiring to allow their ships to operate off local hydroelectrical power while in port.

Like most cruise ports, the shops and galleries are concentrated right near the docks, and passengers will be pleasantly surprised at the peaceful pace of life on the streets if they take the time to walk up and out of the downtown commercial district.

The Mt. Roberts Tramway operates from right by the main cruise ship docks, **See P. 161** Another good stop close to the docks is the Taku Fisheries Ice House, at the south end of the main downtown dock complex. This is an active fish processing facility with ice being delivered, boats unloading, as well as a great seafood restaurant and retail shop with some excellent seafood products.

Shopping: North Franklin Street, which runs right past

the cruise ship docks, is the main passenger shopping venue. If you are at all interested in Native Alaskan Art, I recommend taking some time in the art galleries here.

Mendenhall Glacier: If there ever were a reason for the "See it before it melts," motto used by some travel agents, it is this glacier. **See P. 160**

Whale Watching: A special mention should be made of the whale watching excursions operating out of Auke Bay. There are usually resident populations of both killer and humpback whales in nearby Lynn Canal, and this tour has an excellent record of finding them and many passengers have reported seeing humpbacks bubble feeding or breaching on these tour boats. Red Dog Saloon: If you're looking for a colorful spot for a modestly priced pub food style meal, stop in at the Red Dog Saloon, right on North Franklin, about two blocks from the tramway station. With sawdust on the floor, banjo playing and rustic decor, it's full of local flavor.

SOME JUNEAU EXCURSIONS

Mendenhall Glacier Explorer	Whale Watching & Wildlife Quest
Mendenhall Gl. & Salmon Hatchery Tour	Mendenhall Glacier & Whale Quest
Original Alaska Salmon Bake	Whale Watching & Orca Point Lodge
Underground Juneau	Mendenhall Glacier Float Trip
Rainforest Garden	Glacier View Sea Kayaking
A Taste Of Juneau	Mendenhall Glacier Canoe Adventure
Guide's Choice Adventure Hike	Taku Glacier Lodge Flight & Feast
Dog Sled Summer Camp	Pilot's Choice Ice Age Exploration
Gold Panning & History Tour	Mendenhall Glacier Helicopter Tour
Glacier View Bike & Brew	Four Glacier Adventure By Helicopter
Rainforest Canopy & Zipline Expedition	Glacier & Dog Sled Adventure By Helicopter
Mountain Zip & Rainforest Bike Ride	Dog Sledding On The Mendenhall
Juneau Sportfishing Adventure	Custom Hummer Adventure
Juneau Fly-Out Fly Fishing	
Juneau Steamboat Cruise	
Photo Safari By Land & Sea	
Alaska's Whales & Rainforest Trails	

Zipline excursions are becoming mainstream - this is the rainforest zip excursion which is actually partially over what used to be the old Treadwell Mine. These excursions start with a lesson, so don't feel like they are only for younger or experienced folks.

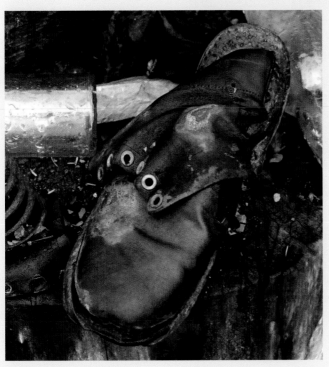

Top: Juneau waterfront, circa 1930, The present tram station is below the tanks lower left. Above the tanks are the piles of mile tailings - ground up rock left after the gold is extracted, that eventually created much of the land on which much of lower downtown Juneau is built. Opposite page top: In the Last Chance Mining Museum, the largest air compressor Inglersoll Rand ever built (powered by a 355 rpm 2200 volt 180 amp electric motor) waits for miners that will never return. Opposite lower left: Little is left of the massive Treadwell Mining Co. except for ruins hidden in the forest and this structure, once part of a pumping station. Opposite lower right: an air powered mining engine slowly being taken over by the forest. Left. Treadwell worker's shoes and debris found on the beach, Douglas Island, just across from the cruise ship docks.

Unusual Excursions

Captain John George, here with Frankie Miller, operates his wood fired steam launch "Susanna" out of the float at the north end of the cruise ship docks. The "Susanna" closely resembles the "Marion", the first steam ferry carrying passengers between Juneau and Douglas Island as early as 1886. During the harbor cruise, Captain George gives a unique presentation on gold mining and early Juneau history.

Tickets are available on any Princess Cruise ship, at the Mount Roberts Tram or by calling him at (907) 723-0372.

Take the Flume Trail back to downtown.

Explore Behind Town!

At the Last Chance Basin Museum

Flume Trail

Gold Creek

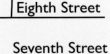

Basin Road

1/2 mile to Perseverance Trail and Last Chance Basin Museum

This is really a great walk!

Look for this sign... then right at the bottom, left at the cemetary, over the bridge....

Eighth Street

Seventh Street

Sixth Street

Trail to Mt. Juneau

Fifth Street

Gold St.

From the miles of tunnels, cold air blows out an old mine entrance on the Perseverance Trail...

Many of these streets end in stairs leading up to houses on slopes too steep for cars. Imagine lugging your groceries up these stairs in winter!

Franklin St.

past Sara Palin's old house (before she resigned as Governor) and downhill all the way back to the ship!

Don't miss the Crab Shack!

Cruise ship dock

159

Mendenhall:
See it before it melts...

*Shrinking Mendenhall -
this is the same spot
in 2009 (top) and 1950
(bottom.)*

Mendenhall - about 25 minutes from downtown Juneau is a great short and inexpensive excursion (bus from downtown is $14 roundtrip) that allows you to get real close to the ice. Usually there are enough icebergs on the lake to allow you to almost touch one - you might have to wade!

But if there were ever a "See it before it melts" place, this would probably be it. Check out the glacier position in these two photos, taken from the same spot, 55 years apart. The pace of its retreat has accelerated noticeably in recent years. 1950 photo by F. Garland Swain.

160

Tram Tip:
Go in the evening...

Top: Looking Northwest from the top - Gastineau Channel, with airport center right, Auke Bay beyond and in the distance the mountains on the west side of Lynn Canal, which capture the snow that creates Glacier Bay.

What to expect: A trail system leads from the top station around the nearby higher hills and peaks, offering both short and much longer hikes. Tip: if you elect to walk back to downtown, be sure you have good footwear and are in good shape - it's all down hill, but occasionally steep and slippery. And tell someone where you're going...

Also on top are a restaurant, espresso stand, gift shop and theater that plays a good 20 minute documentary on Tlingit Native culture.

Tip: if it's a clear evening - go up and stay as late as you can and still get back to your ship. The evening vistas and light are particularly dramatic.

Cost: $17.50- ticket good all day

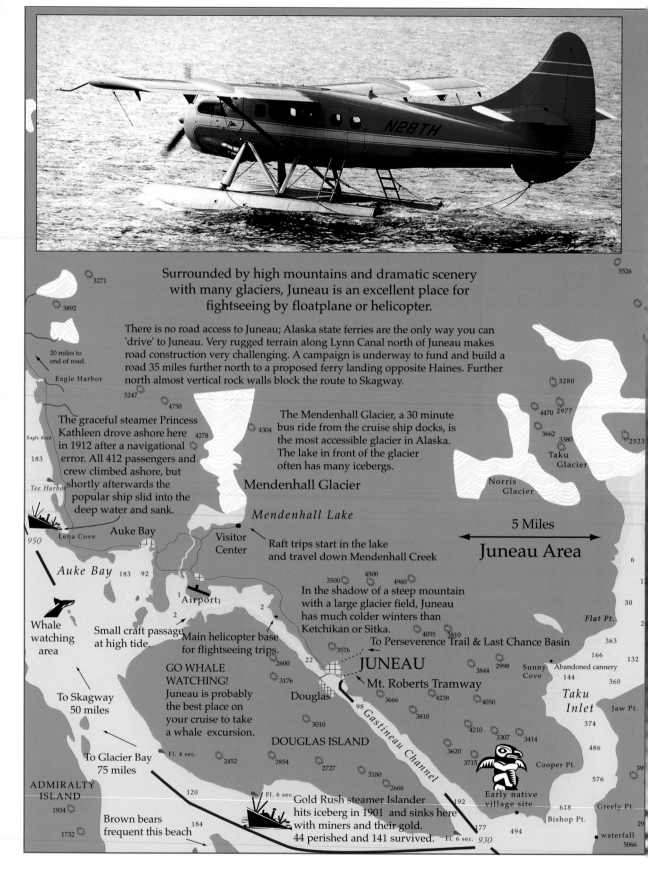

Surrounded by high mountains and dramatic scenery with many glaciers, Juneau is an excellent place for fightseeing by floatplane or helicopter.

There is no road access to Juneau; Alaska state ferries are the only way you can 'drive' to Juneau. Very rugged terrain along Lynn Canal north of Juneau makes road construction very challenging. A campaign is underway to fund and build a road 35 miles further north to a proposed ferry landing opposite Haines. Further north almost vertical rock walls block the route to Skagway.

3271

3892

20 miles to end of road.

Eagle Harbor

5247

4750

The Mendenhall Glacier, a 30 minute bus ride from the cruise ship docks, is the most accessible glacier in Alaska. The lake in front of the glacier often has many icebergs.

5526

3280

4470 2977

3662

3380

2523

Taku Glacier

The graceful steamer Princess Kathleen drove ashore here in 1912 after a navigational error. All 412 passengers and crew climbed ashore, but shortly afterwards the popular ship slid into the deep water and sank.

4278

4304

Eagle Rock

183

Tee Harbor

Norris Glacier

Mendenhall Glacier

Mendenhall Lake

950

Lena Cove

Auke Bay

Visitor Center

Raft trips start in the lake and travel down Mendenhall Creek

5 Miles

Juneau Area

Auke Bay 183 92

6

Whale watching area

1 Airport₁

2

2

Small craft passage at high tide.

Main helicopter base for flightseeing trips.

In the shadow of a steep mountain with a large glacier field, Juneau has much colder winters than Ketchikan or Sitka.

3500 4500 4960

Flat Pt.

30

2

4055 3810

To Perseverence Trail & Last Chance Basin

363

To Skagway 50 miles

GO WHALE WATCHING! Juneau is probably the best place on your cruise to take a whale excursion.

2600

3176

Douglas

22

3576

JUNEAU

Mt. Roberts Tramway

3844 2998

Sunny Cove

166

Abandoned cannery

144

132

360

To Glacier Bay 75 miles

Douglas

DOUGLAS ISLAND

3010

3666

98 Gastineau Channel

4238

3810

4050

Taku Inlet

Jaw Pt.

374

ADMIRALTY ISLAND

Fl. 4 sec.

2452

2854

2727

3180

4210

3307

3414

3620

3715

486

Cooper Pt.

576

39

1934

120

Fl. 6 sec.

Gold Rush steamer Islander hits iceberg in 1901 and sinks here with miners and their gold. 44 perished and 141 survived.

Early native village site.

618

Greely Pt.

Bishop Pt.

29

1732

Brown bears frequent this beach

184

2666

192

177

494

Fl. 6 sec. 930

waterfall

5066

Treadwell's Lesson: Don't Mine the Columns

The great mine at Treadwell was a huge enterprise. In its heyday, around 1900, it was the largest gold mine in the world, employing 2000 people, many of whom shuttled over from Juneau every day.

But while the Juneau mines back in the Silver Bow Basin behind and above downtown, honeycombed the hills with tunnels and shafts, some far below sea level, the Treadwell mine was situated just a few hundred feet back from the salt water of Gastineau Channel.

And the search for the best ore led out, under the channel, under the salt water, deeper and deeper. As in any mine, there was always water coming in, but a steam pump pretty much took care of that.

This style of mining was called room and pillar - wide horizontal areas called levels were excavated with pillars left to hold up the immense weight of the earth above. As the mine got deeper, the pillars got more and more massive.

Then the ore being brought up became leaner and leaner - containing less ore. Of course, there was plenty of good ore left in those pillars.. so the operators began shaving them.. thinner and thinner. They should known better, or if they didn't, should have listened to the mine. For it didn't like it at all: rooms and levels started collapsing as early as May 1913, when the 880 foot level collapsed into the 1100 foot level. A few months later, an internal collapse shook town, knocking dishes off shelves... Plenty of warning.

But they kept digging and shaving those pillars. By April of 1917, the ground was regularly shifting and buildings were settling, etc. On the 20th, a ladies pool party had to be abruptly canceled when the steel pool suddenly developed a crack from the settling of the ground under it and all the water was sucked out.

Around 11 PM on the 21st, families emerging from a movie heard an odd sound: rushing water. An unusually high tide had eroded a channel into the "Glory Hole," the big entrance to the mine. Within a few minutes billions of gallons of water were pouring into the complex in an unstoppable flood. The pressure of the air being forced out blew out the buildings on top of mine shafts and more than 2,000 feet below, miners were running to make it to the elevators. It was truly amazing that everyone got out. But the huge mine was history, and the army and World War I was waiting for many of the miners who had lost their jobs.

Misty Sitka

Consider yourself lucky if your ship stops here. The lack of a cruise ship dock (all but very small cruise ships anchor and use lighters to send passengers ashore) and a slightly off the beaten path location make for a much more mellow downtown environment than you will find in other major Alaska cruise ports. Additionally, Sitka is easily your most historic port.

When Juneau was woods and snow and Ketchikan was a summer village of the Tlingit people, Sitka residents enjoyed theater, fine wines, and all the riches that the sea otter trade provided her Russian residents.

It was a trade based on the unwilling participation of the native people. In the Aleutian Islands, for example, the Promyshlenniki, as the Russian fur traders were called, had no qualms about destroying villages if the Aleut residents didn't catch and skin sea otters for them.

At Sitka, the proud Tlingit people cared little for the Russians, and in 1802 they destroyed the first Russian outpost, north of the present town site. Two years later the Russians returned with three ships and many Aleut mercenaries in kayak-like bidarka boats. Finally routing the Tlingits, the Russians reestablished Sitka on the site of the Tlingit village, Shee Atika.

For much of its Russian history, Sitka's leader was Aleksandr Baranov, who established schools for the Tlingits and made Sitka the trading capital of the northwest coast. These were prosperous years when Sitka was

Mt. Edgecumbe, looming over town, is dormant, but a few April Fools' days ago, pranksters flew a chopper of old tires up the crater before dawn and set a big smoky fire...

Right: the New Archangel Dancers perform traditional Russian folk dancers.

the busiest port on the entire west coast of North and South America.

Fortunately for the Americans, the Russians' enlightenment didn't extend to conserving the valuable fur resource, for once the sea otter had been slaughtered almost to extinction, financial reverses made the Russians willing to sell Alaska to the United States for $7.2 million, about 2 cents an acre, which they did in 1867.

After the Americans took over, Sitka slowly evolved into a sleepy fishing and logging town until World War II when the Japanese invasion of the Aleutians triggered a massive navy operation near where the site of the present airport, with a huge influx of sailors.

In more modern times, Sitka's economy pretty much depended on the big plywood mill out in Sawmill Cove, and commercial fishing. The closure of the mill in 1992 was a substantial financial blow. But instead of languishing, Sitka experienced sort of a slow renaissance based on the arts, and to a lesser degree, tourism.

Today, having missed the booms and busts of the gold rush, Sitka, way out on the ocean side of Baranof Island, is the cultural center of Southeastern

Top: Sitka, circa 1890.
SITK 3770 Collection of Sitka National Historical
Park

Master carver Tommy Joseph at the Sitka National Historical Park visitor center. Visitors are welcome in the carving room. Right: part of the centennial pole, raised in 2011 and carved by James and a team of native carvers, definitely has some non traditional elements.

Top: A kayak instructor goes over paddling and safety skills before a group of paddlers hits the water. Bottom: A troller heads out from Sitka Harbor.

Alaska. Yet Sitka offers more than museums and vistas:

Go fishing: If you have any inclination to try for a salmon or halibut, Sitka is an excellent place to go out on one of the charter vessels. The city's unique position on the outside coast and the strong runs of king and silver salmon make the chances of getting a fish here very high. Such a trip is also an opportunity to see close-up the dramatic coast of Alaska and its sea life and wildlife.

Jet boats: Advances in vessel design and propulsion at Sitka's Allen Marine have made an unusual experience available here: the high-speed jet boats. Propelled by water jets (essentially large pumps) rather than conventional propellers, these impressive craft allow passengers to travel quickly to places such as Salisbury Sound, 25 miles north of town. The abundant wildlife populations make it likely you'll see a whale, bear, or sea otter (today protected by federal law).

The Sheldon Jackson Museum: In his travels through the state as education agent, Dr. Jackson acquired a remarkable collection of native art and historical artifacts. Even if you have seen other such displays, you will find this collection unusually complete and worth seeing. The Aleut and Eskimo exhibits are particularly fascinating, with material

such as rain gear made of walrus intestines.

Alaska Raptor Rehabilitation Center: A place where injured hawks, falcons, owls, and eagles (mostly eagles) are cared for, this volunteer-run facility lets visitors view the dramatic birds close-up.

Sitka National Historical Park: If you didn't get to Totem Bight or Saxman at Ketchikan and want to get a good view of totem poles, this is a close-to-downtown opportunity to do so. Set among trees in a dramatic walk along the shore, the 15 totems are "recarves" of poles collected from Prince of Wales Island at the turn of the century. Cedar totems have a life of about 100 years outside exposed to the elements.

The Russian Bishop's House and St. Michael's Cathedral: Both downtown, these are culturally rich elements of Sitka's Russian period. The Bishop's House is the original 1842 structure; the cathedral is a replica of the one destroyed by fire in 1966 (much of the artwork was saved).

Top left: a fishing boat crew "hanging" a new seine net. Top right: a great grey owl at the Alaska Raptor Rehabilitation Center. Very reclusive in the wild, these are gorgeous birds, and the center is probably your only chance to get a close up look at one! Bottom: Sitka is known as the arts and cultural center of Southeast Alaska. This young woman plays her fiddle at the dock to welcome visitors.

SITKA FINE ARTS CAMP
ON THE SHELDON JACKSON CAMPUS

The campus at Sheldon Jackson College, to the right of where cruise passengers come ashore, houses not only a college, but an arts camp, and most notably, the Sheldon Jackson Museum, housed in the octagonal building. Inside, in the somewhat dark and cluttered main room is a remarkable display of native art and artifacts collected in the early 1900s. If Jackson hadn't been a collector, much of this wonderful art would have disappeared. Tip: if you have one, bring a flashlight to see into the display cases.

Top: A small cruise ship, the Mist Cove, tied up at the Seafood Producer's Co Op dock. Left: The Alaska Pioneers Home overlooks the harbor, a fitting view as many of its residents are retired fishermen. Alaska operates six of these homes across the state. Bottom - home on tiny island, just west of the bridge to the airport.

173

Peril Strait: If you are on a small cruise ship, or Alaska ferry that transits Peril Strait on your way to Sitka, make sure you get up early (arriving vessels will often go through around dawn.) The tide runs so strongly here - actually sucking the big Coast Guard buoys underwater at times - that safe passage is only possible at slack water, around the time of high or low tide. It is particularly scenic, as it winds between many islands, both in Peril Strait, but also in Neva and Olga Straits, closer to Sitka. The narrowest part of the channel is called Sergius Rapids for the powerful whirlpools.

Even modern navigational equipment can't always keep vessels out of trouble: the Alaska ferry *Le Conte* - the ship in this photo - hit a rock here in 2004 and almost sank. Just at the beginning of the busy summer season, it was a huge inconvenience. Electronic glitch? Nope, human error.

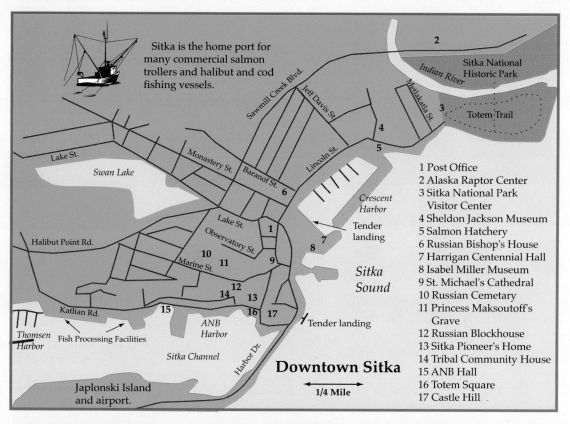

Sitka is the home port for many commercial salmon trollers and halibut and cod fishing vessels.

Sawmill Creek Blvd.

Jeff Davis St.

Indian River

Sitka National Historic Park

2

Metlakatla St.

3

Totem Trail

4

Lake St.

Monastery St.

Baranof St.

Lincoln St.

5

Swan Lake

6

Crescent Harbor

Tender landing

Lake St.

Observatory St.

1

Halibut Point Rd.

10

Marine St.

11

9

7

8

Sitka Sound

12

14

13

15

16

17

Katlian Rd.

ANB Harbor

Tender landing

Thomsen Harbor

Fish Processing Facilities

Sitka Channel

Harbor Dr.

Japlonski Island and airport.

Downtown Sitka

1/4 Mile

1 Post Office
2 Alaska Raptor Center
3 Sitka National Park Visitor Center
4 Sheldon Jackson Museum
5 Salmon Hatchery
6 Russian Bishop's House
7 Harrigan Centennial Hall
8 Isabel Miller Museum
9 St. Michael's Cathedral
10 Russian Cemetary
11 Princess Maksoutoff's Grave
12 Russian Blockhouse
13 Sitka Pioneer's Home
14 Tribal Community House
15 ANB Hall
16 Totem Square
17 Castle Hill

SOME SITKA EXCURSIONS

Russian America History Tour
Russian America & Raptor Center Tour
Sitka Nature & History Walk
Sitka Bike & Hike Tour
Advanced Bike Adventure
Tongass Rainforest Hike
4x4 Wilderness Adventure
Sitka Sportfishing
Wilderness Sea Kayaking Adventure

Dry Suit Snorkel Adventure
Sea Life Discovery Semi-Submersible
Sea Otter & Wildlife Quest
Sea Otter Quest & Alaska Raptor Center
Silver Bay Nature Cruise & Hatchery Tour
Wildlife Quest & Beach Trek
Alaska Up-Close Exclusive Cruise Adventure

Photos from the E.W. Merrill Collection at the Sitka National Historical Park, mostly taken in the late 1800s.

Building the boats: After making it over the passes, the next step for the Klondikers was to cut down trees, saw them into boards, and build crude boats. Then when the lake ice melted, they had to float and paddle down 500 miles of the Yukon River to Dawson and the Klondike Country. The first part included several violent rapids where boats and men were lost.

CANADA

Carcross

Water route to the Klondike
Lake Bennett

Haines Highway connects with Alaska Highway

ALASKA

Gold Rush Trails

Klondike Highway to Alaska Highway

Chilkoot Pass

White Pass & Yukon Route RR

Skagway

White Pass

Dyea (abandoned)

Haines

The Passes - Canada required that all those headed for the Klondike carry a year's food (about a ton) with them. For most prospectors, this meant many backbreaking trips up over the pass, shuttling their supplies to the border checkpoint.

1014N

Proposed ferry dock

High rugged mountains

Chilkat River

The Road - Many Juneau residents yearn for a road to somewhere. (The only road connection is by ferry.) However the proposed road only runs up Lynn Canal to another ferry dock, as the last miles to Skagway is blocked by almost vertical rock walls.

Eldred Rock Lighthouse

990N

Muir Inlet

Glacier Bay National Park

High and rugged with many glaciers.

Passenger Tip - The landscape of upper Lynn Canal is very dramatic. When you leave Skagway in the evening, spend some time with your camera on an upper deck; the views can be spectacular!

Glacier Bay

Lynn Canal

Proposed road

Salmon Cannery

Berners Bay

Excursion Inlet

960N

Present road ends here

Pt. Retreat Lighthouse

JUNEAU TO SKAGWAY

1" = 12 miles

975

950

Auke Bay

Icy Strait

Mendenhall Glacier

Juneau

Taku River

Douglas

Admiralty Island

ALASKA

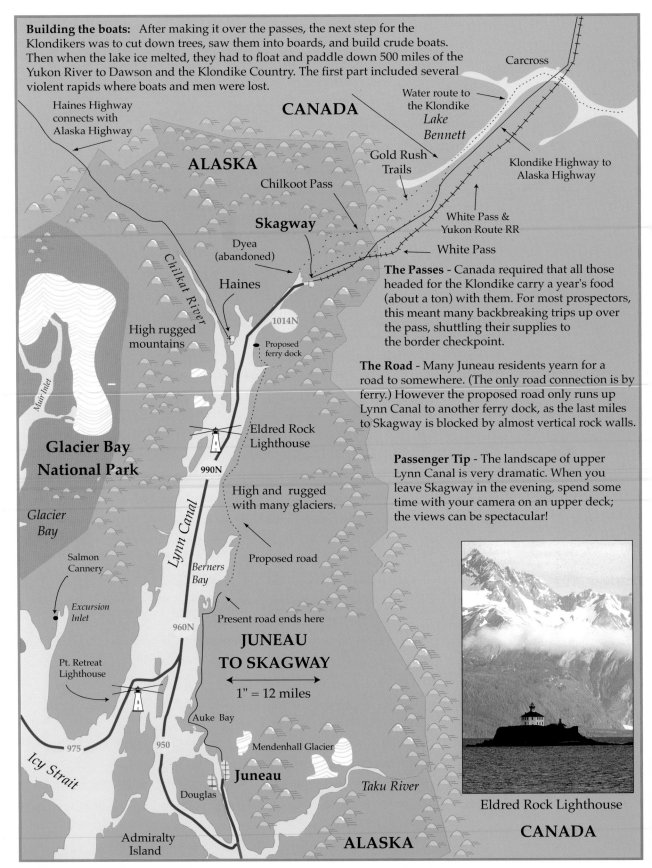

Eldred Rock Lighthouse

CANADA

CHAPTER 4

Where History Lurks
Lynn Canal to Skagway Area, Mile 900 to Mile 1000N

"That country up there didn't look cordial. It made you feel like cutting out the horseplay and saying a prayer for the fellows who wasn't there no more and for the rest of us who didn't know what was ahead, neither."

- Mckeown, *The Trail Led North*

> **Passenger Tip:**
>
> Get up early and stay up late here and go on the upper decks to get a good vista. The landscape is especially dramatic.

Top: looking southwest toward Haines from about Mile 1000N. Bottom: tragedy - the families of these men will never know their fate.

There's a dramatic change in the landscape as your ship enters Lynn Canal north of Juneau. The mountains are higher, the vistas starker, glaciers seem to overhang the water in little cirque valleys.

And it wasn't just the landscape, but the weather as well; Lynn Canal and Chatham Strait, to the south, form a 200 mile long wind tunnel for the wet North Pacific lows sweeping up from the ocean and the cold Arctic highs pushing down from Siberia and the Alaska interior. Especially in the fall, there would hardly even be a break between systems. Weatherbound fishermen in Auke Bay would catch a ride out to the shore by Pt. Lena to get their grim weather forecast: row after row of nasty looking grey bearded seas rolling down the canal.

The bottom here is littered here with the pieces of two of the finest steamers to travel north, both

Disaster in the making: the Princess Sophia cradled on the rocks of Vanderbilt Reef, Lynn Canal, on October 24, 1918. Sure that all would be safe until the weather got better, the rescue fleet decided to wait before taking off the passengers. It was a tragic error - the wind came on again hard, a violent blizzard after dark, and drove the Sophia off the reef and into the deep water beyond. Her last message: "For God's sake, come! We are sinking." Of the 343 on board, there were no survivors. ASL p87-1702 Bottom: The octagonal Eldred Rock Lighthouse, at Mile 990N is a major landmark.

belonging to the Canadian Pacific Railroad. First was the *Princess Sophia*. At around 1 a.m. on October 24, 1918, the gold miners and the crews from the ten Yukon River paddle-wheelers aboard the *Sophia* were probably still celebrating. They'd left Skagway a few hours earlier, the rivers freezing up, their season over and the bright lights ahead.

Upstairs in the pilothouse, the atmosphere was anxious. The captain had seen Eldred Rock Light, **Mile 994**, at midnight through the snow but navigation on such a night relied on something called "time and compass." The skipper would calculate from the engine revolutions how fast his vessel was traveling. Taking his course line from the chart and making allowances for the wind and the tidal currents, he would steer until his time ran out, that is, when he should be at the next point of reference.

On that bitter night in 1918, with blowing snow and limited visibility, the next checkpoint after Eldred Rock was Sentinel Island Light, 28 miles away. Over such a distance, a steering error of one degree would put the vessel a half-mile off course.

Sometime around 2 a.m., as her skipper was groping through the snow and trying to see the Sentinel Island Light, the *Sophia* drove her whole length ashore on Vanderbilt Reef. Fortunately the rocks cradled her, and there was no need to try and launch lifeboats on such a rotten night.

By first light a rescue fleet was standing by: the *Cedar, King and Winge, Estebeth, Elsinore,* and others. But it was decided to wait until better weather to evacuate the passengers and crew.

It proved to be a tragic mistake. In the late afternoon, the northerly began to blow with renewed fury and the rescue fleet was forced to seek shelter in a nearby harbor. Darkness came with driving snow and bitter wind.

Roaring down the canal, the wind caught the *Sophia*'s high exposed stern, driving her off the reef, ripping open her bottom and sending her into the deep water beyond. There was time for one desperate radio call: "For God's sake come! We are sinking." In the morning only her masts were above water: her 343 passengers and crew drowned in the northwest coast's worst maritime disaster.

Thirty-four years later, miscalculation of a course change drove the graceful *Princess Kathleen* ashore at Lena Point, **Mile 956**; her passengers were more fortunate. They climbed down ladders to the rocky beach and watched the favorite of all the Alaska-run steamers slide off the rocks and disappear into deep water.

On the east side of Lynn Canal, at around **Mile 980N** look for what remains of the old mining settlement of Comet. Behind it in the vicinity of Lion's Head Mountain is a highly mineralized area, with several old abandoned mines. A project at the old Kensington Mine, is being developed. The mining company promised a low environmental impact operation; however part of the tailings will be dumped into a nearby lake, angering local commercial fishermen and environmentalists. Whether or not the mine can successfully operate without any adverse environmental impact will be a critical test of the idea of balancing development and natural resource protection.

Top: Beyond the shelter of Cannery Cove and a fleet of gillnetters and a fish buyer, a powerful fall storm sweeps up Chilkat Inlet. Bottom: Pacific salmon die after spawning and attract many scavengers!

The spot that looks like a New England village at **Mile 1012N** is Fort William H. Seward, sometimes known as Port Chilkoot. Decommissioned after World War II, it is now part of the city of Haines, just to the north, and offers a variety of cultural activities.

Haines, until the highway to Skagway was completed in 1979, was the only town in southeastern Alaska with a road that went anywhere (it connected to the Alaska Highway). Today it is rich with Tlingit culture and is especially known for the dramatic fall migration of bald eagles that feed on Chilkat River salmon.

Few large cruise ships stop here, but if you want a refreshing change from the congestion of Skagway when the big ships are in town, there is a foot ferry over to Haines. You'll find a nice path from the dock along the shore to a very laid back town with some great views overlooking Lynn Canal. If your ship does stop, there is usually a kayaking excursion as well as a trip down the Chilkat River, usually by big inflatable rafts.

If you're up for some exercise, groups have taken the

Mellow Haines is a very different visitor experience than any other town visited by big cruise ships in Southeast Alaska. Opposite top: braided channels in the mouth of the Chilkat River. Opposite bottom - there is an obvious pride here that this is not a town dominated by the cruise industry. P. 184 - At the Hammer Museum, and inside the regalia closet at the Native Arts Center, Port Chilkoot.

kayaking trip reported a really good experience, getting up close to sea lions, etc.

Just to the west of town, over the hill, is the mouth of the Chilkat River. Here it winds through an ever changing landscape of islands and sand bars. In Tlingit, Chilkat means 'winter storage container for salmon,' which pretty much sums it up - salmon runs continue here into late winter. The presence of so many fish attracts the largest collection of bald eagles anywhere. Haines markets itself as Valley of the Eagles and has a festival, usually in early November, when typically there are **three or four thousand eagles** hanging out along the lower river, chowing down on the carcasses of chum salmon that have spawned and died. The river excursion takes you lazily right through the heart of this. In summer, of course, there aren't as many eagles, but there still are plenty.

If you haven't seen totem carving up close, the native cultural center on the south side of Port Chilkoot has an ongoing totem carving project.

Haines is also a pretty good place to bike - there are bike rentals as well as bike tours. If you're on your own, ask for the road to Cannery Cove. It's very scenic - with glacier hung mountains over the inlet. And if you want to get to Skagway, just jump on the *Chilkat Express*, a short walk to the left as you get off your ship in Haines. It's just a 30 minute trip to a totally different world.

We are Not like Skagway

We get very few ship dockings
We are self-owned shops
We are not owned by the cruise lines

Please help support Haines!

Why Juneau isn't getting a road out...
any time soon.

You may already know that the only way in or out of Juneau is by boat or plane. In recent years, however, there has been a movement to build a road north along the east side of Lynn Canal. It would run about 40 miles north to connect to Skagway, where there is a road up the valley that connects with the Alaska Highway in Canada's Yukon territory.

Like most things Alaskan, there are strong feelings on both sides of the issue. Juneauites would love a road and it would open up the Juneau hospitals for Skagway and Haines residents, as well as bringing 80,000 or so more visitors and their RVs to a city of 31,000 that might have 10,000 cruise passengers visiting on a five ship day. Definitely a mixed blessing there...

But the biggest challenge is simply the landscape - almost vertical in places, with many well established avalanche chutes, it would be hugely expensive to build, and expensive to maintain in the winter. Plus it wouldn't even go all the way - but simply to a ferry dock a few miles from Haines.

Of course, the lawyers love this one - several lawsuits have been filed and the state's environmental impact statement was possibly headed for the US Supreme Court, unless cooler heads prevail..

Someday, there may indeed be a road out, but no one is really sure when.

Mushers. Alaska.

The Gold Rush: How many struck it rich?

On Chilkoot Pass

"Sixty-Eight Rich Men on the Steamer Portland"

"Not a man has less than $5,000. Some of them have over $100,000"

"Big strikes made by tenderfeet"

"Fortune seemed to smile on the inexperienced."

"Strikes in the Yukon the greatest ever known."

Such were the headlines in the July 17, 1897 Seattle Post-Intelligencer that spread across a depression ravaged country like wildfire. In those days, to a family struggling to keep food on the table and coal in the stove, $5,000 was a fortune, $100,000 riches beyond imagination. The dimensions of mysterious Alaska and Yukon had just began to enter American consciousness, primarily through John Muir's exciting discovery of Glacier Bay just 20 years before.

Left: Above: look at these faces aboard a Gold Rush steamer. UW Thwaites 0394-1286 Top: The infamous "Golden Staircase" at Chilkat Pass in 1897 Above: getting there could be bad; a Gold Rush steamer at Skagway UW15549

Above: The frenzy that the Gold Rush started—steamer Excelsior leaving San Francisco for the"El Dorado of the Yukon," with thousands of jealous well wishers looking on. UW Partridge 7964 Bottom: Prospectors on barge coming ashore in Skagway. The ships didn't wait for high tide to make it easier. As one Klondiker put it, "They had to get back and pick up another load of suckers..." UW La Roche 380

But the part that electrified struggling men all across America and Canada was that most of the rich men coming out to tell their stories had gone in as inexperienced "tenderfeet," with no more knowledge of Alaska, the Klondike, or gold mining than the average midwest sodbuster or eastern factory worker.

Desperate people see what they want to see; most didn't read the small print, at the end of the article that started with "GOLD! GOLD! GOLD! GOLD! splashed across the front page. "They attribute their success to "lucky strikes," and aver that thousands of people will rush to the Yukon valley in the next year or two, and after undergoing great privations and hardships, will probably return broke in health and finances."

And so they came, from all parts of the country, from all walks of life, fixated on finding the gold that would transform their lives. First to Seattle, where the waterfront was a frenzied marketplace of merchants hawking their supplies to eager men with their family's savings in their pockets.

A Gold Rush fleet was rushed into service. Some were

older, tired ships, operated by unscrupulous owners wanting to get in on the Gold Rush frenzy. Overloaded and pushed into dangerous weather, several didn't make it and were lost. For the tens of thousands who came north during the Gold Rush years, upper Lynn Canal represented the last easy miles of their journey to the diggings.

As you enter Taiya Inlet at **Mile 1,014N** from Seattle, imagine yourself at the crowded rail of a ship like the *Queen* or the *Victoria* in the fall of '97, jostling for your place with hundreds of other Klondikers, looking out through a snow squall, trying to get a glimpse of what lay ahead. There is but an hour or two before you must put on your pack, get the boxes and sacks of your "outfit" (a year's worth of supplies) ready to unload, and step out into the wind and the cold and whatever fate had in store for you.

> **"Them days it was every man for hisself. The faster a boat could get out of there, the sooner it could get back to Seattle or Vancouver and pick up another load of suckers.** A man shipped his gear at his own risk. If he didn't get his stuff off the beach before the next tide, it was just his hard luck. No one else done no worrying about it."
>
> - Monte Hawthorn, in *The Trail Led North*

Ready for the next phase of their journey: freshly built boats and Klondikers on Lake Bennett, Spring, 1898. These boats were built from planks hand sawn from trees around the lake. AMRC b64-1-43 Below: Display in Gold Rush museum in Seattle, just a few blocks from where these scenes occurred: merchants eagerly selling supplies, some of dubious value or quality, to the gold frenzied crowds.

How the wealthy traveled to the Klondike: a paddlewheeler winching itself through Five Finger Rapids on Yukon River. UW Hegg 501

The snow clears, and a cold and cheerless sun shines on as bleak and unfriendly a landscape as you've probably ever seen. The mountains rise vertically out of the water; there doesn't even seem to be a beach. The chatter of the crowd fades as all look at the mountains and what lies ahead.

For those in the first wave in 1897, there were no wharves. Most gold seekers unloaded their outfits from steamers onto lighters–shallow-draft barges. If the tide was up, the lighters took you right in to shore. If it wasn't, the lighter got as far as the flats and you had to cross 200 or 300 yards of sand and mud to get to shore. Many had brought animals and staked them out with their piles of boxes and gear while they made the first trips across the flats to shore.

Some weren't familiar with the big tides in the northern fjords of Alaska. They rested, perhaps, after lugging their first load up the beach, and visited with others about what they might expect in the rough-hewn town, visible through the snow, and hiked back to find their outfit underwater, their animals drowned. Few were really prepared for the rigors of that journey, or the true nature of the gold country.

For most of the hundred thousand or so who came north in 1897 and 1898, their Gold Rush experience had three phases. The first was often the hardest: the passes.

The mountain wall that lay between the salt water of upper Lynn Canal and the edge of the Yukon had but two routes over it: Chilkoot Pass and White Pass.

The most powerful image from '97 and '98 is the long line of climbers, each bent with his load, on the steps cut into the ice on Chilkoot Pass. At the top lay the Canadian border and the North West Mounted Police. No one could pass without a year's supplies, about 1,000 lbs.

Wealthy men hired porters, but most just carried it all up themselves, load by backbreaking load, caching it at the top and hoping no one would rob them before they got back. A solid stream of upward-bound men filled the steps. If you wanted to rest, you stepped off to the side, but when you wanted to get back in, you had to wait for a gap in the line; it was that crowded. By 1898 cable tramways could carry your gear over the pass for a fee, but the men in the first wave had only their feet.

Down the other side from the summit was Lake Bennett and after that it was the boats and the rivers. They were 50 miles from salt water, but there were another 500 to the gold country. Arriving in winter, the men camped on the shore, cut down trees, whipsawed them into planks and built boats, and waited for the ice to melt to launch their boats and begin the journey:

"Some leaked, some didn't steer. They had lots of things wrong with them. But a lot of the boats, made of whipsawed lumber, had beautiful lines

The epic of the Gold Rush - how many men would have kept going if they knew what awaited them once they left the comfort of the ships and headed up over the trail? And the sad part was this: few struck it rich; almost all the good claims were staked even before the first wave arrived in the summer of 1898.

THE LUCKY FEW

With no convenient banks, many miners simply brought their gold south with them. One woman, hearing that her husband might be coming home to Seattle on the steamer, brought their children to meet it, hoping he'd have enough money to buy them groceries (he'd been gone six months and they were out of money). He staggered down the gang-plank under the weight of his duffel and its 116 *pounds* of gold.

MOHAI 404

Spring 1897, the next stage of the epic journey begins as the ice melts and the many waiting boats begin their long river journey. Note the wrecked boat, hung up on the rock in the center of the picture. UW Hegg 227
Below: For some, the challenge of The North - the cold, the difficult conditions, was simply too much:

"..he was setting there in the middle of the road talking to himself... He looked plumb played out. He never seen us, he just went on talking to himself..." Christine Cox drawing

and sailed as pretty as anything I ever did see on the Columbia. Yes, sir, that was an expedition, that fleet of boats getting ready to set out from Lake Bennett, come spring of '98."

—Martha McKeown, *The Trail Led North*

The trip became a journey of true epic proportions. Down the canyons and through the rapids they came, some capsizing or breaking up; the survivors trying to hitch a ride with the next boat that had room. The wealthier switched to Yukon steamers as soon as the river got wide enough, but all were heading for Dawson Creek and the last phase of their epic sagas: the diggings.

But for most, only disappointment awaited them. The best claims were staked before most of the gold seekers arrived. Many who started north gave up before they got to the Yukon. Only half who made it staked a claim. Just a very few struck it rich. Most found some kind of work in Dawson City or in the diggings, made a little money, and moved on.

Yet their adventure transcends time. All experienced the powerful drama of **The North**. Those who returned to the lower 48, even penniless, brought back stories and memories to entertain generations of breathless children and grandchildren.

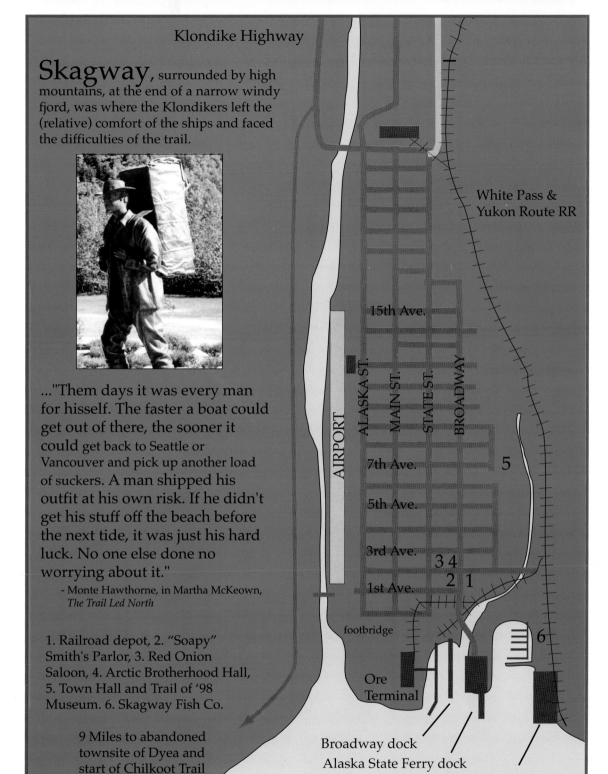

Klondike Highway

Skagway, surrounded by high mountains, at the end of a narrow windy fjord, was where the Klondikers left the (relative) comfort of the ships and faced the difficulties of the trail.

...."Them days it was every man for hisself. The faster a boat could get out of there, the sooner it could get back to Seattle or Vancouver and pick up another load of suckers. A man shipped his outfit at his own risk. If he didn't get his stuff off the beach before the next tide, it was just his hard luck. No one else done no worrying about it."

- Monte Hawthorne, in Martha McKeown, *The Trail Led North*

1. Railroad depot, 2. "Soapy" Smith's Parlor, 3. Red Onion Saloon, 4. Arctic Brotherhood Hall, 5. Town Hall and Trail of '98 Museum. 6. Skagway Fish Co.

9 Miles to abandoned townsite of Dyea and start of Chilkoot Trail

White Pass & Yukon Route RR

15th Ave.

ALASKA ST.

MAIN ST.

STATE ST.

BROADWAY

AIRPORT

7th Ave.

5

5th Ave.

3rd Ave.

3 4

1st Ave.

2 1

footbridge

6

Ore Terminal

Broadway dock

Alaska State Ferry dock

WP&YR RR dock

1022 m. to Seattle via Inside Passage

SKAGWAY

Occasionally in the early 1970s my commercial salmon fishing buddies and I would travel up to Skagway for the weekend, when fishing was closed around Haines, around 15 miles south. The merchants were thrilled to welcome our group, kept their shops and restaurants open late for our business. Dust blew in the empty streets, or if the Alaska state ferry was in, perhaps a few dozen visitors wandered around. It was definitely sleepy.

This isn't what you'll find today. If you come by cruise ship, you'll probably arrive with eight or ten thousand other visitors to a town with perhaps 825 permanent residents.

Yet surprisingly, this town still retains its charm and the ghosts of the men who passed through in the epic Gold Rush that essentially put Alaska on the map still walk these streets.

As much as anything that kept the turn of the 20th century buildings intact – Skagway essentially was built between 1897 and 1900 – was the weather. Buildings that

Above: Evening light, downtown Skagway. The building on the right is the Arctic Brotherhood Hall, a major meeting place for those headed for the legendary gold fields in 1897-8. Below: a classic coach waiting for guests at the Skagway Gold Rush Cemetery, east of town.

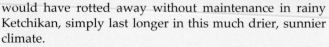

Merchants wasted no time - this classic Alaska gift shop started with the Gold Rush in 1897, and was recently acquired by a jewelry chain, who thought better of the totems... Below: Before the big chain gift shops came to town, Skagway had some wonderful locally owned small stores.

would have rotted away without maintenance in rainy Ketchikan, simply last longer in this much drier, sunnier climate.

But it is the drama of '97 and '98 that fills this town. Skagway blossomed for but a few years, lawless and rough, then almost disappeared.

The gaunt-faced men have passed through to whatever fate **The North** had in store for them. The town the boom built at the jumping-off place for the Klondike remains, looking much as it did in 1897 and 1898, when some 80 saloons and many professional women were anxious to serve the lonely men on the trail north.

Today, Skagway offers a unique experience to visitors. Even the vegetation is different from the rest of Southeast Alaska, because the town is under the influence of the harsher temperature extremes of the interior instead of the milder, cloudier maritime climate elsewhere in the region. Some of the native craftwork available here, especially of ivory, is truly excellent.

Note: Only ivory harvested by Native carvers in accordance with federal regulations may be sold legally. Make sure to get a export/transit permit if you buy ivory and plan to transit Canada on your way home. You'll need it to bring the ivory into the

United States.

If Skagway's your last stop and you've saved your shopping until the end, you're in luck, the density of shops, particularly jewelry shops (their website, Skagway.com lists 17...) equals that of any other town on your cruise.

Shopping's great, but make sure you take some time between your excursion if you take one, and shopping, to just walk around town, get a sense of the place and of the drama that took place here.

A good place to start is the Gold Rush **National Historical Park Visitor Center**, on the water side of downtown in the White Pass and Yukon Route Railroad station. It gives a great overview of the Gold Rush saga, as well as being in the train station for the WP&YR RR, which is fascinating just by itself. The town of Skagway also operates its own visitor's center, in the restored and very dramatic **Arctic Brotherhood Hall,** with its 10,000 or so nailed on pieces of driftwood, probably the most distinctive building in all of Alaska. The Fraternal Order of the Arctic Brotherhood constructed this hall and at least another in the Yukon Territories as a social and cultural organization to fur-

A guide explains the workings of a gold dredge on the Skagway River. Above, the Three Friends Dredge, circa 1950. Environmental regulations would make it difficult or impossible to operate such dredges today. UW17960

ther the interests of the miners. It grew to have substantial political muscle as well. being an early advocate for more political power for Alaskans to manage their own affairs locally rather than through Washington, DC.

Pick up a copy of the walking tour map at the **AB Hall.** It's got directions up to the Gold Rush Cemetery, the **Trail of '98 Museum**, and other points of interest. It's definitely worthwhile to walk around with the map as your guide. The hike to Lower Dewey Lake (3 hrs. RT) has a steep stretch at the beginning, but then flattens out for a very pleasant walk.

Of course, Skagway's signature hike is up the old **Chilkoot Trail**, followed by so many of the men of '98. This is way, way more than a pleasant stroll; more like a grueling 4-5 day epic, and that's in summer, not in the depth of winter with the poorly insulated clothing of the day and 1000 pounds of gear to pack over the summit. If you start up the trail, think about this: many of the men who took it made a dozen or more trips back and forth to ferry their loads if they couldn't afford to hire a native porter to help them.

One good way to see the old trail is an excursion combining a hike up the first few miles with a raft trip back down the river to Dyea. Skagway and Dyea boomed together, but today only Skagway remains, primarily because of the railroad and the docks quickly constructed there. (The tide flats at Dyea were almost a half mile wide on a big low tide, a long, long, way to carry your gear in multiple trips.)

What's interesting about Dyea is this–today the ruins seem really far from the water even at high tide. As it turns out, the land used to be much lower, and hence the water much closer. But as the glaciers that used to cover this whole area thousands of feet deep had only receded recently (well, maybe 10,000 years earlier) the land was experiencing 'glacial rebound' to the tune of about a half to three quarters of an inch a year–enough to lift the land 6-7 feet since the Gold Rush and push the waterline back considerably in that flat river delta.

Just renting a bike downtown for a few hours is also a pretty mellow way just to explore the town and surrounds. The 10 miles out to Dyea is a pretty nice ride, but at least in 2005 much of the road was unpaved and though we loved the free tour by a ranger around the old townsite, we were really glad when a kind driver offered to run us up to "the top of the hill." (Which was most of the way back to Skagway.)

The helicopter excursions that operate out of near the waterfront are a good way to see the dramatic landscape as well as the Chilkoot Trail. There are a number of different variations most of which include a landing on top of one of the nearby glaciers and a chance to walk around. If you're ready to dig deep and have never been around dog teams, there is an excursion that includes a dog sled ride. The dogs get really excited then the choppers land and they know that they will be on the trail soon!

Save some time at the end of the day to drop in to one of the local watering holes like the Red Onion Saloon, where a lot of the Klondikers tipped a few before they hit the rugged trail. If you want a bit more local color, try Moe's Frontier Bar, between 4th and 5th. Another highly recommended spot is The Skagway Fish Company, located by the small boat harbor out near the Railroad docks.

But most of all, try and take a few moments to think about the men who came, in the fall of 1897, and walked these streets and prepared for the obviously difficult challenges ahead. And the Skagway of those days was very very different from the cheerful busy place you'll encounter. By all accounts it was a grim place full of hard men.

Top: Summer housing for workers here gets creative. Below: driftwood door at the Arctic Brotherhood Hall, now the Skagway Visitor's Center. Opposite top: This is a great place for some helicopter sightseeing. Bottom: keeping the tracks clear in winter was a huge job, even for a plow like this!

TAKE THE TRAIN!

Top: And this is in May! When the Klondikers got to Skagway, the snow in the passes was way deeper than this! Opposite top: control levers in an old gold dredge.

After struggling for years after the end of the Gold Rush, hauling ore from Yukon Territory mines to the ore terminal at Skagway Harbor allowed the railroad to modernize and operate for over 8 decades. But when mineral prices slumped in the early 1980s, the railroad had to suspend operations and Skagway lost an important source of revenue and outlet to interior Canada.

Fortunately by 1988, enough visitors were coming by cruise ship that the railroad could reopen, focused on providing rides aboard classic restored railroad cars for visiting passengers.

After carrying just 37,000 travelers in 1988, the railroad has become the most popular visitor attraction in Alaska, carrying 431,000 passengers in 2006!

It operates daily on a number of schedules - train up, bus down, train to summit and back, train to Lake Bennett and back (longer.) In my view, as long as you just get on the train and up the mountain, it doesn't make much difference which itinerary you take. But take the train!

SOME SKAGWAY EXCURSIONS

Skagway & The Dangerous Days Of '98
Klondike Summit & Liarsville Experience
Klondike Summit, Bridge, & Salmon Bake
Historical Tour & Liarsville Salmon Bake
Skagway's Original Street Car
To The Summit
Experience The Yukon
White Pass Scenic Railway
Best Of Skagway
Klondike Scenic Highlights
Delectable Jewell Gardens
Deluxe Klondike Experience & Rail
        Adventure
Alaska Garden & Gourmet Tour
Yukon Jeep Adventure
Horseback Riding Adventure
Klondike Bicycle Tour
Rainforest Bicycle Tour
Klondike Rock Climbing & Rappelling
Alaska Sled Dog & Musher's Camp
Chilkoot Trail Hike & Float Adventure
Glacier Point Wilderness Safari
Glacier Lake Kayak & Scenic Railway
Dog Sledding & Glacier Flightseeing
Glacier Discovery By Helicopter

Heli-Hike & Rail Adventure
Alaska Nature & Wildlife Expedition
Remote Coastal Nature Hike
Takshanuk Mountain Trail By 4x4
Eagle Preserve Wildlife River Adventure
Chilkoot Lake Freshwater Fishing
Wilderness Kayak Experience
Skagway's Custom Classic Cars
Glacier Country Flightseeing

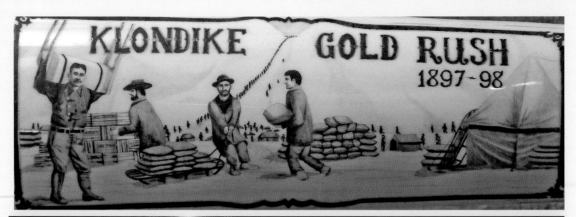

KLONDIKE GOLD RUSH 1897~98

SIBERIA 19 21 · E. CAPE · Pt. HOPE · ALASKA 1923
WRANGEL ISLAND ORDEAL 1921 to '23 · V. STE

ALEXANDER ·DGE'S H. GROVE. W.F. McNE· ·DGE'JE·
ALONG ·OKOVITO· S·
·THONY·
·CL·
THE PRINCESS SOPHIA DISASTER of 1918

THE ORDEAL OF GREGORY AYAC
BERING STRAIT 1 2 3 4
ALASKA
1 DIOMEDES
2 WALES
3 IKPEK
4 EAR ·
KING ISL.

Dennis Corrington's
Ivory Museum

If you want to see some unique Alaska Native art, don't miss Dennis Corrington's Ivory Museum - in the back of his shop on Broadway and 5th. When Dennis was a boarding school principal in the 1960s, often, in the summer, he would go out to visit his students at their homes in remote native communities. Asked to bring hard to get supplies, he was often paid in carved ivory, as the cash economy still hadn't reached there.

Developing a deep interest in Alaska Native art, he eventually set up a store in Skagway, both to sell art, but also to showcase some of the more unique pieces he had collected. The walrus tusks on these pages have been decorated with Alaska history scenes by the same scrimshaw technique used by the crews of whaling ships on the bones and teeth of sperm whales. Dennis travels regularly to visit carvers he has met over the years and bring back their best work.

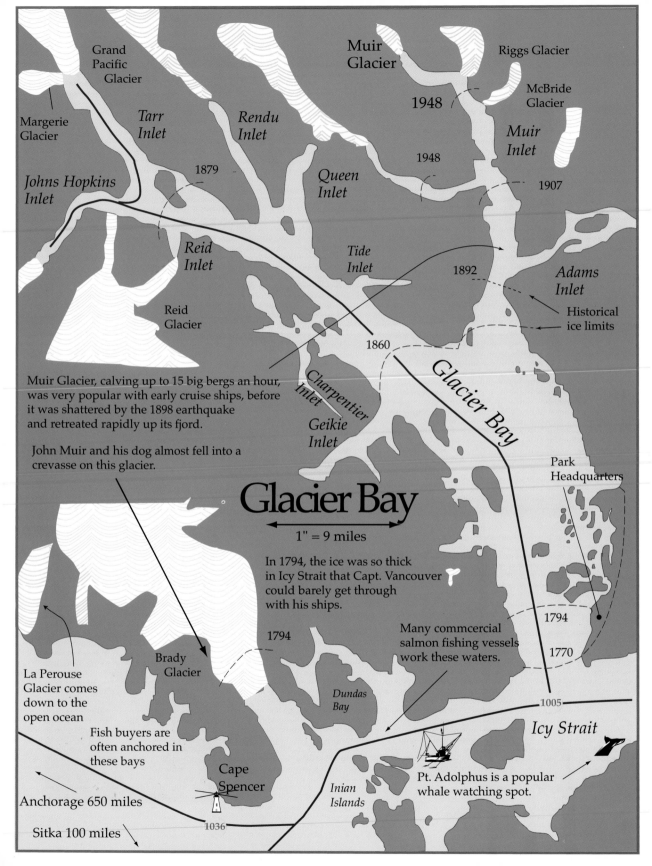

Grand
Pacific
Glacier

Muir
Glacier

Riggs Glacier

McBride
Glacier

Margerie
Glacier

*Tarr
Inlet*

*Rendu
Inlet*

1948

*Muir
Inlet*

*Johns Hopkins
Inlet*

1879

*Queen
Inlet*

1948

1907

*Reid
Inlet*

*Tide
Inlet*

1892

*Adams
Inlet*

Historical
ice limits

Reid
Glacier

1860

Glacier Bay

Muir Glacier, calving up to 15 big bergs an hour,
was very popular with early cruise ships, before
it was shattered by the 1898 earthquake
and retreated rapidly up its fjord.

*Charpentier
Inlet*

*Geikie
Inlet*

John Muir and his dog almost fell into a
crevasse on this glacier.

Park
Headquarters

Glacier Bay

1" = 9 miles

In 1794, the ice was so thick
in Icy Strait that Capt. Vancouver
could barely get through
with his ships.

1794

Many commcercial
salmon fishing vessels
work these waters.

1794

1770

La Perouse
Glacier comes
down to the
open ocean

Brady
Glacier

*Dundas
Bay*

1005

Icy Strait

Fish buyers are
often anchored in
these bays

Cape
Spencer

Pt. Adolphus is a popular
whale watching spot.

Anchorage 650 miles

*Inian
Islands*

Sitka 100 miles

1036

CHAPTER 5

Into The Ice

Glacier Bay to Cape Spencer, Mile 975 to Mile 1035

"This spacious inlet presented to our party an arduous task, as the space between the shores on the northern and southern sides, seemed to be entirely occupied by one compact sheet of ice as far as the eye could distinguish."
-George Vancouver, *A Voyage ...*

This was Vancouver's Lieutenant Joseph Whidbey looking east to Icy Strait from near the entrance to what is today Glacier Bay. The Strait was completely choked with ice and appeared to be impassable. To the north, the bay was closed by "compact solid mountains of ice, rising perpendicularly from the water's edge." Glacier Bay didn't exist; it was solid ice.

A month or so after this discovery, Vancouver and his men finished their three summer exploration of the Northwest Coast and determined that there was no ice free Northwest Passage back to the Atlantic. They headed off to England around Cape Horn. And Glacier Bay disappeared into the mists of time for some 80 years.

Top: Dawn Princess in Queen Inlet - when glaciers recede, a very austere landscape is created.. Below: commercial fisherman and family at Margarie Glacier.

The Tlingits, of course, from the nearby village of Hoonah, and the Chilkats, hunted seals and had found that often the best hunting was on the very edge of the ice, where seals would often go to calve and nurse their pups. So it is very likely that during this period, if the ice had been receeding, they would have been moving north with it, setting up hunting camps in Glacier Bay, but leaving no written records. Then in 1877, an explorer, Charles Wood, seeking to climb Mt. St. Elias, entered a now much bigger Glacier Bay and noted he had to travel 40 miles to reach the ice front. While there, he stopped at a Tlingit seal hunter's camp and recorded another bit of information that gives an insight to the ice's rapid recession. The chief, around 30 years old, said that within his lifetime the whole area around them had been solid ice.

This was startling: it meant that **within that relatively short period of 30 years, 10 or 20 cubic miles of ice had disappeared.** What caused such a great recession of the vast ice sheets during this period—some earlier version of global warming? No one really yet knows, but events in the late

Muir Glacier in 1890

Since then the Muir has retreated almost 30 miles.

1890s suggest substantial seismic activity in the Glacier Bay area. As these events were to prove, earthquakes seem to have the ability to shatter the ice in glaciers. Where such glaciers face the water, they will calve off immense amounts of ice after an earthquake, causing them to recede rapidly.

The modern history of Glacier Bay really began in October of 1879, when John Muir, a noted naturalist and early preservationist, left Wrangell by canoe with a missionary friend, and three native paddlers. He had heard rumors of ice mountains in Alaska and had come to find out for himself.

He had neither gore-tex nor fleece; his canoe was overloaded, and the route was one today's kayakers probably wouldn't even attempt at that time of year. They paddled west through Sumner Strait, up through Rocky Pass (Keku Strait) and across Frederick Sound to follow the west shore of Admiralty Island north. Their canoe was small, the waters big. When they'd finally crossed the choppy seven mile stretch of open water between Kuiu and Admiralty Islands, his chief paddler told him he hadn't slept for days worrying about it.

On they came, through Chatham and Icy Strait. As they traveled, the youngest native, Sitka Charley, told Muir he'd hunted seals as a boy in a bay full of ice and

Top: Muir Glacier was the premier destination for early cruise ships, calving icebergs at a rapid rate. Plus passengers were invited to go ashore and climb up! Below: in his first trip in 1879, Muir traveled in a native canoe with frightened native Tlingit paddlers. Christine Cox drawing.

209

What's wrong with this picture? (Other than no life jacket...) Well the danger for small craft around icebergs is that as they melt, their center of gravity changes, and they can topple over without warning. See drawing below.

thought he could show Muir the way.

Muir was skeptical. Sitka Charley said the bay was without trees and that they'd need to bring their own firewood. The other paddlers, in all their lives throughout the region, had never seen a place without firewood.

They came to a bay cloaked in fog and storm. Sitka Charley became uneasy; the bay was much changed, he said, since he had seen it before. Even Vancouver's chart, a copy of which Muir so much relied upon, failed them, showing only a wide indentation in the shore.

Fortunately, they found a group of natives hunting seals and staying in a dark and crowded hut. One of the men agreed to guide them, and northward they paddled, off the chart and into that astonishing bay that had been birthed from the ice almost within their lifetimes.

The weather got worse and Muir's paddlers wanted to turn around:

"They seemed to be losing heart with every howl of the wind, and, fearing that they might fail me now that I was in the midst of so grand a congregation of glaciers, I made haste to reassure them that for ten years I had wandered alone among mountains and storms, and good luck always followed me, that with me, therefore, they need fear nothing. The storm would soon cease and the sun would shine to show us the way we should go, for God cares for us and guides us as long as we are trustful and brave, therefore all childish fear must be put away."

—John Muir, *Travels in Alaska*

So on they went, camping in rain, on snowy beaches, pushing farther and farther, only glimpsing the vastness and grandeur of the land.

Finally Muir climbed the flanks of one of the mountains just as the clouds passed, and he gazed, stunned, at the grandeur and the size of the many-armed bay that was revealed below him, full of slowly moving ice.

When the party headed back, the lateness of the season was evident. Each morning before they reached Icy Strait, the ice was frozen a little thicker, and the men had to cut a lane for their canoe with an axe and tent poles.

Muir's description of his time in Glacier Bay are

Steamer Queen at Muir Glacier, about 1890. This graceful liner was one of the first to regularly bring visitors to Glacier Bay. Passengers could go ashore by small boat and climb ladders up to the top of the glacier. Imagine the Park Service allowing that today! Photo courtesy of Dave Bohn.

some of the shining icons of Alaskan literature:

"Then setting sail, we were driven wildly up the fiord, as if the storm wind were saying, 'Go then, if you will, into my icy chamber; but you shall stay in until I am ready to let you out.' All this time sleety rain was falling on the bay and snow on the mountains; but soon after we landed the sky began to open. The camp was made on a rocky bench beneath the front of the Pacific Glacier, and the canoe was carried beyond the reach of the bergs and berg waves. The bergs were now crowded in a dense pack against the discharging front, as if the storm wind had determined to make the glacier take back her crystal offspring and keep them at home."

—John Muir, *Travels in Alaska*

After Muir's discovery and powerful writings about what he'd seen, the bay soon became one of the premier sights of the Western Hemisphere, and a regular stop for steamers such as the *Ancon*, the *Idaho*, and the *Queen*.

For many of the early steamer excursions, part of the trip was taking the ship's boats to shore and if conditions permitted, taking groups to the top of the glacier itself to climb around amongst the crevasses!

The destination was Muir Glacier, the face of which was an ice cliff towering above the decks of

Below: Joe and Muz Ibach built a cabin by Reid Glacier, above, around 1940, laboriously bringing in good dirt for a garden. They had a gold claim in the hills high above the glacier. But it never yielded much and friends suspected they just loved the glorious scenery and isolation. Bruce Black photograph

the approaching steamers and calving up to 12 icebergs an hour.

"The Muir presented a perpendicular ice front at least 200 feet in height, from which huge bergs were detached at frequent intervals. The sight and sound of one of these huge masses of ice falling from the cliff, or suddenly appearing from the submarine ice-foot, was something which once witnessed was not to be forgotten. It was grand and impressive beyond description."
—Fremont Morse, *National Geographic,* January, 1908

LOOKING FOR WILDLIFE

Glacier Bay is actually one of the best opportunities to see bears and goats from your ship. However, you will need the strongest binoculars you can lay your hands on!

For bears, there are a couple of places to look. After about mid summer, there will be lots of berries on the slopes around the bay. So "glass" these hillsides carefully. What you will be looking for will be something that looks like a black spot that appears to be moving as it forages through the berry bushes. Another good place to look is along the shore, especially at low tide, as bears will forage for clams, crabs, etc.

Mountain goats will be on the higher, steeper hillsides, and will be the white dots slowly moving!

Look for bears both on the hillsides above Glacier Bay as well as along the shore. Photo by Ki Whorton
Looking for mountain goats—from the deck you will see what look like moving white dots. Binoculars will reveal the goats, grazing on amazingly steep slopes. Below: How many mountain goats can you find?

Look for seals on ice flows around Glacier Bay. There are some concerns about the effect of vessel traffic on the seal population in the Bay, and John Hopkins Inlet is usually closed for part of the summer in order not to disturb seals there.

YOUR DAY IN GLACIER BAY

In order to allow each visitor to have the richest experience of the Park's unusual beauty, cruise ship visits are limited to two or less daily. Park Rangers will board your ship to offer information and give presentations. A free informative map will be placed in your state-room the night before. To get the most out of your Glacier Bay visit, I suggest stopping by the onboard ranger station with any questions, attending the presentation in the theatre, as well as viewing the video, *Beneath the Reflections* on stateroom TV. If young children are with you, consider the Junior Ranger program.

The 1899 Earthquake—At midday on September 10, 1899, as he was waiting for lunch at his salmon saltery in Bartlett Cove, now site of Glacier Bay National Park headquarters, August Buschmann was surprised to see his trunk come sliding across the floor at him. Moments later, the cook's helper came running into the building, frightened. He had been up on the hill at the native cemetery as the ground started to heave around him, and he thought the dead were coming to life.

The earthquake shattered the front of Muir Glacier and others, and within 48 hours Glacier Bay was a mass of floating ice so thick that ships could not reach the saltery at Bartlett Cove for two weeks. Icy Strait filled with ice, making Dundas Bay, ten miles to the west, inaccessible.

It wasn't until the following July that the steamer *Queen* ventured close enough to Muir Inlet to see what had happened. The bay was still full of ice; only by picking their way along the shore west of Willoughby Island could they make any progress. The closest they could get to Muir Glacier was ten miles; the rest was solid ice.

Hidden behind a fleet of icebergs, Muir Glacier commenced a rapid retreat up the inlet; today the face is 25 miles north of where Muir found it in 1879.

Usually large cruise ships travel up the west side of Glacier Bay, often slowing or stopping to allow passengers a good view of Reid Inlet. Next to the north is the entrance to Johns Hopkins Glacier, very active in recent years, and the outgoing stream of ice is often so thick that ships often do not enter, for fear their propellors would contact ice pieces large enough to damage them. Additionally, seals use the ice flows in this inlet to birth their pups. During the period when they are actively birthing pups, ship traffic is prohibited here.

However, while seal activity is the thickest in the inlet itself, you are apt to see seals, and perhaps even with their pups on ice flows anywhere in Glacier Bay, so be sure to have your binoculars ready whenever you leave your cabin in this area.

Then most big ships will travel up and stop as close to Margerie Glacier and Grand Pacific Glacier as they can. In recent years there has been less ice here than John Hopkins, and ships are often able to approach fairly closely.

WATCHING FOR CALVING ICEBERGS

Things to look for that might signal calving is approaching include a section of much bluer ice than the rest of the glacier face and or small showers of ice and snow tumbling into the water, and cracking and rumbling sounds. Also remember that the ice face often extends several hundred feet beneath the surface, and icebergs the size of houses or larger can break off from the underwater part of a glacier and suddenly surface (another reason for small craft to give icebergs a good berth.)

Next page: photo by Dan Kowalski of iceberg in Le Conte Bay, near Petersburg.

Whales In Glacier Bay

It's not clear why whales breach. Theories include trying to get rid of barnacles, establishing dominance over smaller males at mating time, and just wanting to have a bit of fun! Kay Gibson photo. Below: This pod of whales came so close to where we were watching from the promenade deck of the Dawn Princess that we could hear their trumpeting and smell their rotten fish breath when they surfaced close to us!

Glacier Bay has traditionally been a good spot to see humpbacks and other whales, so be sure to have your binoculars with you on deck and remember to keep a sharp eye peeled. Your ship will have a naturalist, but there may be whales that he or she doesn't see.

Another good spot for whale watching is **Point Adolphus, Mile 1000**, directly south of the entrance to Glacier Bay. Your Captain may query the local whale watching boats and if he gets a report of sightings there may take a loop through before continuing on his course.

I was here in 1997 on the *Dawn Princess* when our Captain got a tip and, taking a loop through, spotted a group of humpbacks and let us ship drift, in hopes they might come closer. Regulations require big ships to keep a quarter of a mile away from whales, but in this case, after we stopped, the whales swam right over to us. I was on deck seven, the promenade deck, and had my camera handy as our fascinated group peered over the rail as the pod of five big humpbacks moved closer and closer until they were almost directly below where we were standing!

I had seen humpbacks blow at a distance before, but this time they were close enough to hear their distictive 'trumpeting' when they exhaled after a long dive. This was actually too close as their breath was bad, bad, bad!

A Tale of Inian Cove

I spent much of my 19th summer in this cove, south of **Mile 1025,** buying fish from big native-owned fishing boats aboard the 75' tender *Sidney*. These were powered with immense, straight eight Chrysler Royal gas engines. One of my jobs was to keep them tuned and running smoothly. In these 58-footers, the fo'c's'le, or crew area, was right in front of the engine, and as I worked, replacing spark plugs and filing points, I could hear the natives talking. Sometimes they spoke their native language, but other times it was English. They spoke of the fishing, but also of the legend of Lituya Bay, over and beyond the ice mountains to the north. I didn't understand all that was said, but they seemed to be speaking of an angry spirit that sometimes lashed out, creating great waves that washed away villages.

Once or twice that summer, ice drifted into the anchorage at night, a powerful, almost magical experience for me:

"**August 17, 1965, Inian Cove**. Something woke me in the night, and I sat up in my bunk, wondering what it was. And then it came again, a faint but insistent scraping, as if another boat had drifted down on us in the night. I stumbled out on deck and, there, eerily lit by the three-quarter moon, was a big iceberg, moving gently down our port side, pushed by the tide. Its irregularly shaped top was even with my head; I reached out to touch it, to try and retrieve some of the gravel clearly visible within its pale, translucent flank. The gravel had been scraped off a canyon floor, dozens of miles away, hundreds of years before I was born. But the ice was hard, its contours softened by melting. My hand could find no purchase, and after a moment the berg moved away in the tide.

"Outside the point I saw a ghostly armada moving in the seven-knot current of North Inian Pass: eight or nine little bergs, maybe a thousand tons each, showing as big as medium-sized boats above the surface. In the moonlight they seemed to glow as if lit from within. I wanted to wake my shipmates, but then the tide pushed the bergs around the corner and they were gone."

A cruise ship and a zipline at a cannery? What would the old-timers have said???

ICY STRAIT POINT

Top: Hold on tight; the zipline here is the longest of its kind in the world, 5,330' long and with a 1330' vertical drop. Six riders can zip at once, and at one point you are almost 300' above the cannery with a spectacular view out to Icy Strait, Port Frederick, and your ship. Other excursions include a Hoonah bike tour, wildlife and bear watching expeditions, a forest/nature tram ride, salmon sports fishing, flightseeing over nearby Glacier Bay, Tlingit dancing and a wild Alaska seafood cooking lesson/meal. Photos courtesy Icy Strait Point.

Opening its doors for the first time in 2003, Icy Strait Point is unique among Alaska cruise ports–ship visits are limited to one at a time, and the facility–a renovated cannery next to a Tlingit native village is surrounded by wilderness. If you've cruised Alaska before, you know how congested the other towns can get with four or five ships in port at once, so making a visit here is a welcome change.

Passengers come ashore by lighter to the cannery dock where there is a museum, cafe/restaurant, and numerous shops. Cannery life was a major cultural and economic element in coastal Alaska and this is an excellent chance to get a close look. There are walking trails around the site and additionally there is a shuttle bus to nearby Hoonah, the largest Tlingit village in Alaska. The facility is owned by a native corporation and the richness of Tlingit culture is a strong element throughout.

Icy Strait Point is located in Port Federick, just across Icy Strait from the entrance to Glacier Bay.

Left top: Hoonah around 1900. Left bottom: Hoonah Cold Storage. Commercial fishing is a major activity here. This page - bottom left: Icy Strait Point visitors with a power block and a salmon purse seine net. Bottom right: Icy Strait Point - the town is about a mile east of the old cannery. Top right: on the nature trail - this pleasant and easy walk through the rain forest is truly spectacular. It starts at the cannery and ends at the Landing Cafe, where you can get a meal and watch the dramatic endings of the zipline riders.

To Seward
Whittier
College Fjord
Prince William Sound

1480

Columbia Glacier

Many salmon gillnet vessels operate in the remote Copper River delta area. Marketed as Copper River salmon, the early sockeye run here fetches very high prices in restaurants and to fishermen.

Cape Hinchinbrook

1380

Valdez

ALASKA

Cape St. Elias is a major landmark and a spectacular sight at dawn, when most northbound cruise ships pass it. Have your camera ready!

Cordova

Copper River

Gulf of Alaska

Cape St. Elias

1310

• Katalla

Bering Glacier

With many peaks over 10,000', this part of the Alaska coast has been nicknamed "The roof of North America." Mt. St. Elias, at 18,008 feet, dominates vistas here and seems to loom over the coastal lowlands.

UP THE GLACIER COAST
Cape Spencer, Mile 1036 to
Cape Hinchinbrook, Mile 1380

W N S E

Cape Yakataga

1250

Icy Bay

1220

▲ Mt. St. Elias 18,008'

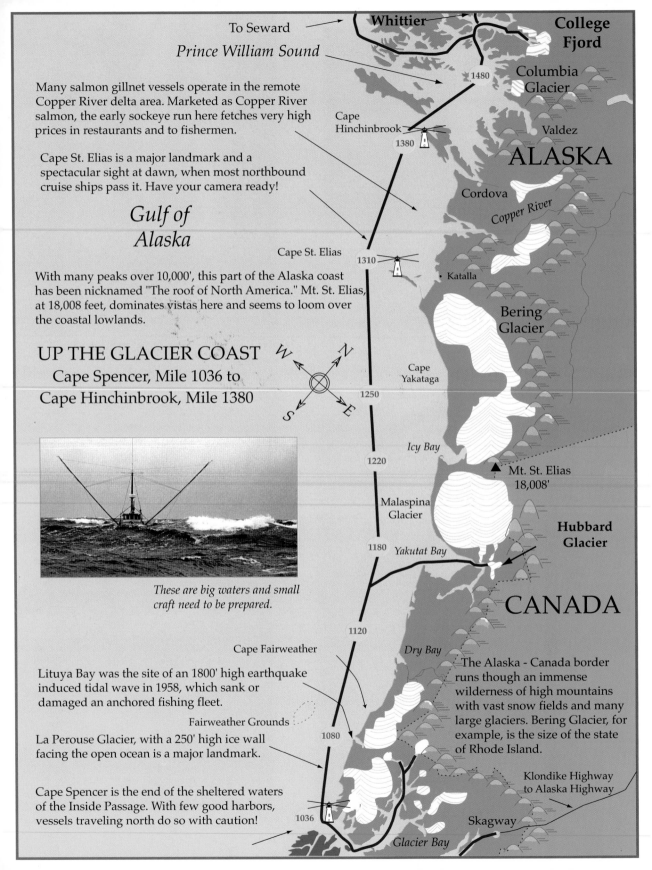

These are big waters and small craft need to be prepared.

Malaspina Glacier

1180   *Yakutat Bay*

Hubbard Glacier

CANADA

1120

Cape Fairweather

Dry Bay

The Alaska - Canada border runs though an immense wilderness of high mountains with vast snow fields and many large glaciers. Bering Glacier, for example, is the size of the state of Rhode Island.

Lituya Bay was the site of an 1800' high earthquake induced tidal wave in 1958, which sank or damaged an anchored fishing fleet.

Fairweather Grounds

1080

La Perouse Glacier, with a 250' high ice wall facing the open ocean is a major landmark.

Klondike Highway to Alaska Highway

Cape Spencer is the end of the sheltered waters of the Inside Passage. With few good harbors, vessels traveling north do so with caution!

1036

Skagway

Glacier Bay

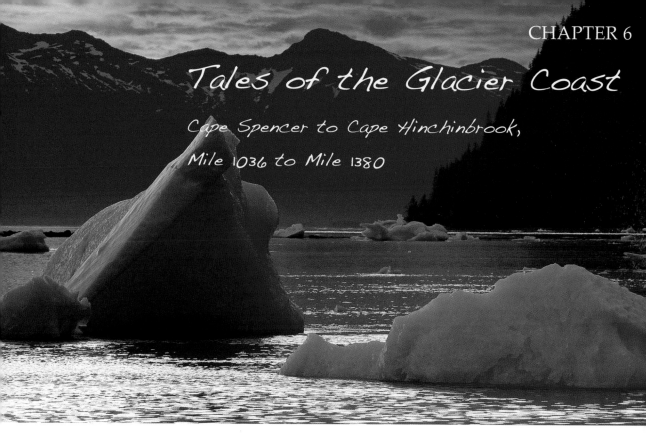

Tales of the Glacier Coast

Cape Spencer to Cape Hinchinbrook,
Mile 1036 to Mile 1380

"We thought it was an iceberg at first, way out past Spencer - you used to see 'em out there sometimes—but then when we got closer, we could see it was a big crab boat. But ... wasn't she iced over! Just like one big hill of ice, with some rigging and antennas sticking out of the top, and ragged pieces of plywood covering where the pilot-house windows were broken out. Pretty soon we could see the crew was all out on deck, knocking off the ice with baseball bats and shoveling it over the side as fast as they could. It gets bad out there..."

—Crab Fisherman Russell Fulton

Top: Near Icy Bay. Dan Kowalaksi photo. Above: a gillnetter/troller bucks into a northerly near La Perouse Glacier.

Mariners tread cautiously here. Gone are the harbors with easy access when the wind blows. (Except for a few bays just north of the Cape.) This is the outside coast: bold, rugged, with few harbors, and backed by the stunning and rugged St. Elias Range. Take the time to go on deck with your binoculars. In North America, only Alaska has a coast like this.

If the coast of British Columbia had been like this, the development of coastal Alaska would have been very different. The myriad harbors and sheltered passages of the Inside Passage allowed very small

Passenger Tip:

Spend some time on an outside deck along this coast especially in the evening or early morning, and bring your camera! On early and late season sailings, northern lights are also occasionally seen here!

Top: early morning off Cape St. Elias. Bottom: evening light off La Perouse Glacier, a major coastal landmark.

craft to travel to Alaska. Many would never have dared head north if their only route was outside, along a coast like this.

Look for **La Perouse Glacier** at **Mile 1060**. With its almost perpendicular 200-300' face, it's an outstanding landmark along this section of coast. This is an active glacier! In some years, like 1997, advancing into the ocean, while just a year earlier receding enough to allow foot passage across the front at low tide.

The land to the east, from the coast up over the Fairweather Range, and into the Yukon Territories of Canada, almost to the Alaska Highway, is for the most part a vast wilderness. It does present, however, an opportunity for kayakers or rafters willing to travel for long distances far from any help or source of supplies.

For the truly brave hearted, the **Dezadeash-Kaskawulsh-Alsek** route includes the infamous **Turnback Canyon**. It was named after the 1898 gold prospectors who tried the Alsek as a route to the interior, had one look at the ten-mile chute of churning icy water and turned around.

This unforgiving canyon has become to kayakers what K2 or Everest is to climbers. A word of caution—sometimes high water and fast currents make this canyon truly impassable and kayakers are urged to have a contingency plan for a helicopter to shuttle them around the canyon.

Three bare, light colored bluffs distinguish Ocean Cape, the entrance to Yakutat Bay, at Mile 1162. This bay is the only really good anchorage for large vessels, in the 350 miles between Cape Spencer

and Prince William Sound. Nevertheless, in very heavy weather, breakers or very high swells have been observed all the way across this 15 mile-wide entrance.

Yakutat, some five miles inside the bay from Ocean Cape, is the northernmost village of the Tlingit Indians, many of whom fish for salmon nearby. It is also a popular destination for sports fishermen who use it as a staging and jumping off place for remote fish camps.

The Roof of North America—East and north of Hubbard Glacier is an area that has been nicknamed 'The Roof of North America'—an immense rock, ice, and snow world with many of the continent's highest peaks. Ten thousand-footers are common here, and there are at least four over 15,000'. Much of this area is the Wrangell St. Elias National Park and Wilderness. This mountain wall catches the eastward flowing moisture-laden air, which falls as heavy snow. The immense weight of the snow pack creates the largest glaciers on the entire Pacific coast. Hubbard Glacier is part of a vast ice mass that extends along a few miles behind the coast in an unbroken line (except for two places) almost to Anchorage, nearly 400 miles away. Today the glaciers have all receded substantially back from the shore, but a century ago, the ice reached the ocean in many places.

Tragedy at Lituya Bay - 21 men from French Explorer La Perouse were lost when their longboats were overwhelmed by the tide rip at the entrance to Lituya Bay, June 1786.

Even today, mariners fear this bay. Not only does it have a very dangerous entrance, but has had a series of tidal waves. The most recent was 1958, when a wave reaching almost 1800 feet high ravaged the bay. Below: the coast near aptly named Dangerous River. Breakers have been seen here several miles from shore.

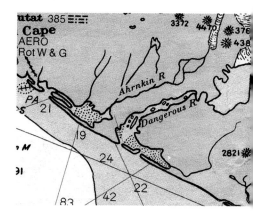

When Glaciers Surge...

Hubbard Glacier, in Yakutat Bay, is another that is regularly visited by cruise ships. Not regulated by the Park Service as Glacier Bay Is, it means that ships that have been unable to get a permit to visit Glacier Bay can still have a chance to expose their passengers to the excitement of getting up close to a glacier.

In April of 1986, Curt Gloyer, a pilot for Gulf Air Taxi, in Yakutat, returning from dropping off a group of climbers, noticed that Hubbard Glacier had surged all the way across the channel, essentially damming the out let of Russell Fjord. He circled lower, just to make sure, amazed at the unusual sight.

This was a event unprecented in recent geologic history, and as soon as word got out, people and groups from all over the world began to flock into town. Many sea lions, seals, dolphins, even perhaps whales were trapped behind the ice dam as the water slowly became fresher and fresher from the rivers and streams that fed into it.

However there was little that the groups could do as slowly the water on the Russell Fjord side got higher and higher, reaching 90 feet more than the ocean on the other side by mid-October. Eventually the pressure of the water was just too much, blowing out part of the ice wall one night. And by the next morning, water was shooting out the hole like a waterfall.

Occasionally, like the Hubbard in 1986, glaciers surge forward. Geologists theorize that occasionally the many streams the flow through a glacier get plugged up and the dammed up water essentially floats the glacier. One of the fastest recorded was Variegated Glacier, which for some reason, surges every 20 years or so, hitting 16 fpd (feet per day..) Not enough to crush you in your tent, but still at over an inch a minute, definitely noticeable

The Fish Train:
On the Situk - Yakutat RR...

SITUK LANDING   YAKUTAT   ALASKA

There's a lot of ways to move fish in Alaska, but this definitely has to be one of the more creative. Here's how it started.

Around 1901, cannery interests had determined that there was a good run at Dry Bay from the Situk River. But.. as the name implies, the entrance to the bay was too shallow for the larger tenders, or fish buying vessels, to cross. Ingeniously the cannery operators built a railroad almost 60 miles from the cannery in Yakutat, to the banks of the Situk River. The first locomotive was reported to be from the old New York elevated railway. Of course, this wasn't your regular railroad. Its schedule changed each day as the fishing boats could only unload at high tide. Fishermen would often ride the train out to Dry Bay on Monday morning and back on Friday afternoon, and locals remember that sometimes the dogs from Yakutat would chase the train all the way to Dry Bay and then chase it all the way back! Photos courtesy Yakutat & Southern Railroad Restoration, Inc

Top: Mt St. Elias looms over much of the coast here. It's also the point where the Alaska border stops following the coastal mountains and shoots arrowlike, directly north to the Arctic Ocean Bottom: Lituya Bay hermit Jim Huscroft was host to many climbing parties, headed to the rugged country to the east. Bradford Washburn photo

Icy Bay, to the north at Mile 1220, has the usual shallow entrance, though in recent years it has been the scene of considerable logging activity. One hundred years ago, the bay wasn't even there—it was filled with a glacier that extended several miles out into the ocean!

These are active glaciers! There is often much ice in the bay, and sometimes icebergs will drift out of the bay and form a regular line of stranded bergs along the outside shore, all the way northwest to Cape Yakataga.

"Cape St. Elias, the south end of Kayak Island, is an important and unmistakable landmark. It is a precipitous, sharp, rocky ridge, about one mile long and 1,665 feet high, with a low, wooded neck between it and the high parts of the island farther north. About 0.2 mile off the cape is the remarkable Pinnacle Rock, 494 feet high."

—U.S. Coast Pilot 9, 1964 ed.

The Copper River emerges from the mountains between Miles and Childs Glaciers, and spreads out into a delta with many islands as it enters the Gulf of Alaska. The river delta and the myriad sand bars are the scene of considerable activity in the late spring and summer with shallow draft salmon gillnetters seeking the well-known Copper River Red Salmon.

Around 10 on the evening of Aug 9,1958, anchored fisherman Howard Ulrich was awakened by his boat rolling suddenly in what had been a peaceful anchorage. He stepped up into the pilothouse and what he saw became etched into his mind forever:

"These great snow-capped giants [the mountains at the head of the bay] shook and twisted and heaved. They seemed to be suffering unbearable internal tortures. Have you ever see a 15,000- foot mountain twist and shake and dance?

At last, as if to rid themselves of their torment, the mountains spewed heavy clouds of snow and rocks into the air and threw huge avalanches down their groaning sides.

During all this I was literally petrified, rooted to the deck. It was not fright but a kind of stunned amazement. I do not believe I thought of it as something that was going to affect me.

This frozen immobility must have lasted for two minutes or longer. Then it came to a dramatic end. It so happened that I was looking over the shoulder of Ceno-taph Island toward the head of the bay, when a mighty seismic disturbance exploded and there was a deafening crash.

I saw a gigantic wall of water, 1,800' high, erupt against the west mountain. I saw it lash against the island, which rises to a height of 320 feet above sea level, and cut a 50-foot-wide swath through the trees of its center. Then I saw it backlash against the eastern shore, sweeping away the timber to a height of more than 500 feet.

Finally, I saw a 50-foot wave come out of this churning turmoil and move along the eastern shore directly toward me."
— Courtesy of Alaska Magazine

This was an earthquake that knocked the needle off the seismograph at the University of Washington, 1000+ miles away. Ulrich and his son were lucky - their boat survived, barely. Another boat, the *Badger*, sank after being carried over the trees of the north spit, its crew survived in a dingy, while a third boat was lost with all aboard.

Above: aerial photo taken a few days after the tidal wave showing where trees were stripped down to bar rock.

A close call at Cape St. Elias

Something woke me around midnight—the motion of our new steel king crabber that had seemed so big tied to the dock in Seattle: slow and loggy, hesitating at the end of each roll, as if it weren't sure it was going to roll back the other way. I dressed and took the steps up to pilothouse and immediately saw the problem.

Ice! A bitter wind had come up, ripping the spray off the ocean and freezing to our hull and rigging. Enough had accumulated to make us so top heavy that capsizing was a very real possibility. This was how vessels died, I suddenly realized.

We dressed quickly in warm clothes and rain gear, and, secured by a safety lines, inched out onto the bow, knocking the ice off with hammers and baseball bats and kicking the pieces over the side.

Once a large sea loomed suddenly out the night and the bow dipped into it and we were suddenly hip deep in the dark swirling water. Our skipper stared out in alarm from the pilothouse through the tiny circle of ice-free glass, and then the bow rose, and sea poured back over the side.

On the back deck, our double stacked pots were a hill of smooth ice and we struggled, hammering and shoveling until we were wet with sweat. Finally our boat seemed to ride a little safer, and we jogged slowly to the shelter of a tiny island, hammering and shoveling all the way.

We pulled the big steel hatch covers off, loaded as many of the heavily iced pots into the holds as would fit, laid the rest flat on the deck, lowered the boom and lashed it to the stern. The icy wind still clawed at us, but there was no sea. When we were finally done I looked around. We were probably the only humans within 50 miles and the vista— frozen islands, shore and mountains, now hidden, now revealed by moon and racing clouds, was unspeakably bleak.

"It's the Copper River wind, boy," the skipper's brother told me in the galley when we were done and warming up. "It just sucks down off the flats and ice after a little sou'west breeze. All that ocean air just gets frozen up there, and all of a sudden decides to roll back to the sea."

"Ah, I shouldn't have let Dad steer at night... that's how it all started—he was almost seventy then and his eyes were starting to go. We were headed up to fish Prince William, and I just laid down for a bit. There was a moon, and not much wind, so I thought he'd be OK. But then the next thing I knew we were in the breakers—he'd just gotten in too close to the beach. The boat started to break up and that was way before survival suits, so we just ended up on the beach in our woolies (long woolen underwear).

"It all happened so quick there really wasn't any time for a radio call. The snow was right down to the water's edge in places—it was late April—so I figured our only chance was to try and make it back to Cape Yakataga. I knew there was at least a lodge or something there...

"It was really tough going—seemed like every mile there was a stream that we either had to wade across, sometimes up to our chests, and all icy snowmelt.

"We slept just huddled together, and then on the afternoon of the second day, Dad told me to leave him—that he couldn't go on any longer... The worst part of it was that we'd lost our snoose (powdered or so called 'smokeless' tobacco) and our chew both with the boat.

"If we hadn't stumbled across an old trapper's cabin, and found some old moldy pipe tobacco that we could chew on, I don't think we would have made it. But we spent the night in there, and each of us got a good chew in our mouths so the next morning life seemed a little more bearable...

"Turns out BP had some sort of drilling operation at the Cape back then, and the first building we came to was the mess hall. It was noon, and we walked in the door, all scratched up, just in bloody ripped woolies and our rubber boots. Everyone turned as we came in the door, and for a long moment, you could have heard a pin drop in there..."

—Dick Kietel, fisherman

Left: Some sort of weird Halloween? Actually this is my crew, practicing putting on their survival suits. Developed in the late 1970s the buoyant and insulating foam suits were quickly embraced by much of the Alaska fleet. Boats with no room to store them sometimes tied the suits to the mast. Top: If hypothermia doesn't get you, the bears might: tracks along the beach north of Dangerous River. Brenda Carney photo

233

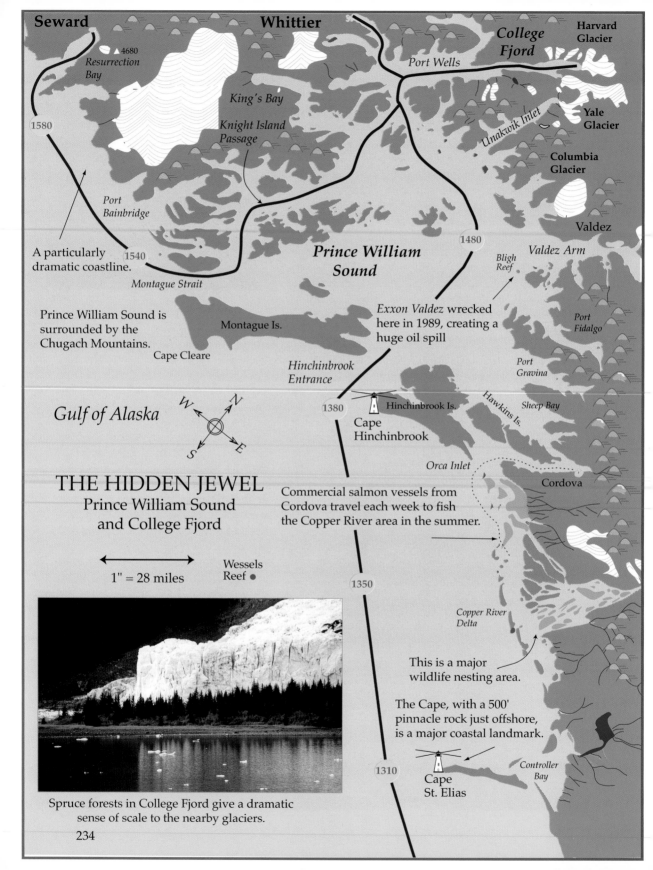

Seward

Whittier

College Fjord

Harvard Glacier

4680
Resurrection Bay

Port Wells

1580

King's Bay

Knight Island Passage

Yale Glacier

Unakwik Inlet

Columbia Glacier

Port Bainbridge

1480

Valdez

A particularly dramatic coastline.

1540

Montague Strait

Prince William Sound

Bligh Reef

Valdez Arm

Prince William Sound is surrounded by the Chugach Mountains.

Montague Is.

Exxon Valdez wrecked here in 1989, creating a huge oil spill

Port Fidalgo

Cape Cleare

Hinchinbrook Entrance

Port Gravina

Gulf of Alaska

N
W   E
S

1380

Hinchinbrook Is.

Hawkins Is.

Sheep Bay

Cape Hinchinbrook

Orca Inlet

Cordova

THE HIDDEN JEWEL
Prince William Sound and College Fjord

Commercial salmon vessels from Cordova travel each week to fish the Copper River area in the summer.

1" = 28 miles

Wessels Reef

1350

Copper River Delta

This is a major wildlife nesting area.

The Cape, with a 500' pinnacle rock just offshore, is a major coastal landmark.

1310

Cape St. Elias

Controller Bay

Spruce forests in College Fjord give a dramatic sense of scale to the nearby glaciers.

234

CHAPTER 7

The Hidden Jewel

College Fjord and Prince William Sound

Cape Hinchinbrook, Mile 1380, is the entrance to many-armed Prince William Sound, an area about the size of some small states. Except for three towns—Cordova, Valdez, and Whittier, and a few settlements, the area is mostly uninhabited, a dramatic island archipelago wilderness with many active glaciers.

If you are on a northbound ship, the early morning light here can be truly spectacular. First light comes real early in the summer, so as soon as you wake up, have a look out your window or if you have an inside cabin, dress warmly and step outside with your camera. The shining 12 and 13,000 footers of the Chugach mountains are sometimes clearly visible from 80 miles away.

Early Explorers: Captain James Cook briefly explored this area in 1778. Setting out from England in the spring of 1768, he made three voyages to become one of the most famous explorers in history. Much of his work was spent in filling in the vast blank space on the map that was the Pacific Ocean. Exploring this section of the coast was to be his last hurrah. Returning to Hawaii, he was tragically killed

With so many glaciers crowded around a single narrow body of water, College Fjord presents a much more dramatic vista than Glacier Bay Bottom: Once hunted almost to extinction, the friendly sea otter has repopulated its range. They especially like to swim on their backs, often placing food on their bellies as they eat.

Top: Sea otter and baby - one of the most enduring parts about these critters is the way they carry their young on their stomach, as they swim on their backs. Below: Today tugs escort tankers on all the way out to Cape Hinchinbrook. Would such a tug have helped avert the Exxon Valdez disaster? Probably not.

Passenger Tip

Have a look to the north when you enter Prince William Sound; you may get a glimpse of Columbia Glacier, the largest and also fastest receding tidewater glacier in Alaska. It was ice from this glacier that forced the Exxon Valdez to alter course and eventually hit Bligh Reef.

in a scuffle with natives in February of 1779.

The Sound teems with sea life such as sea lions, seal, and frequently, humpback whales. Sea otters in particular have made a remarkable comeback. After being hunted almost to extinction, their population has risen to over 100,000 statewide. A particularly good place to watch for them is on small floating ice pieces in College Fjord.

But it is salmon that has been the bread and butter for most fishermen here. During the summer season, tenders or fish-buying vessels spread out to the farthest reaches of the many fjords of the region, to buy fish from both purse seiners and gill-netters. These tenders acted like mother ships, often supplying groceries, water, and fuel for their boats, fishing too far from town to return at night. Many fishermen live in remote communities like Cordova where fishing was about the only game in town.

In the hierarchy of salmon fishermen in Alaska, (There are many salmon fishing districts in Alaska, each with its different style of vessel and gear.) the "Prince William Sound Boys" in the 1980s were doing well. Salmon prices were high, catches were good, and it was a scenic and reasonably calm place to fish. Life was good.

This comfortable world was shattered on March 23, 1989, when a long nightmare began—the oil spill.

The evening of March 23, 1989 was calm, with a lit-

Ice, Oil, and the Exxon Valdez

tle fog, when the *Exxon Valdez* carrying 211,000 tons of North Slope crude oil departed Valdez. A few hours later, Captain Josesph Hazelwood encountered some ice, not uncommon at that time of year. As the vessel was maneuvered around the ice, the tanker hit Bligh Reef, ripping her single skinned hull open.

Within 24 hours some 10 million gallons of crude oil had spread into a slick that covered about 18 square miles. Fortunately, the three days following the grounding were unusually calm—perfect weather for skimming and recovering oil from the surface of the water. Unfortunately, much of the oil spill response equipment promised to be always ready, wasn't available, and the spill spread far and wide, closing many rich fishing grounds. For many fishermen it was their worst nightmare. Exxon organized and funded a huge cleanup effort that fortunately employed many fishermen and chartered their boats.

Since the spill, rules have changed to require double skinned tankers, and a tug escort all the way to Cape Hinchinbrook, but it was essentially closing the door after the horse was gone.

The surprising recovery: in Prince William Sound, nature has shown itself to be remarkably resilient. Many affected sea life populations have returned to previous levels and the area appears to be as pristine as it always was. However neither herring nor salmon have returned to pre-oil spill levels.

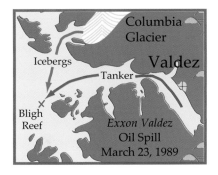

Exxon Valdez Oil Spill March 23, 1989

Top: The beginning of the long nightmare. It was a bitter, bitter experience for fishermen to learn that the oil spill cleanup equipment was not available when it was finally desperately needed. John VanAmeragan photo. As the expression goes, "The only ones who win are the lawyers.." A settlement for punitive damages spent 20 years working its way up to the U.S. Supreme court, only to get slashed... I had been hoping for enough for a little vacation - our fish prices took a big dip that year because of the spill - but the final was more like enough for a good night out on the town..

237

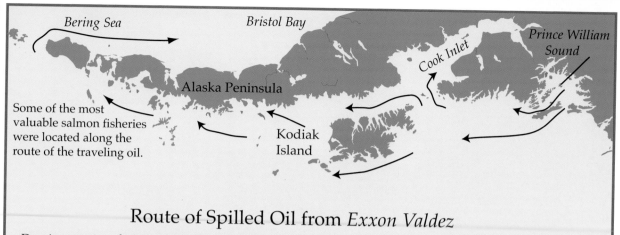

Bering Sea

Bristol Bay

Prince William Sound

Cook Inlet

Alaska Peninsula

Some of the most valuable salmon fisheries were located along the route of the traveling oil.

Kodiak Island

Route of Spilled Oil from *Exxon Valdez*

Despite promises that state of the art containment equipment would be always available in case of a spill, several days passed before that equipment could be readied and brought to the scene of the great spill. By that time it was too late; the oil had congealed, becoming very hard to collect, and, traveling westward with the currents, closed commercial fishing areas along the way. For many commercial salmon and herring fishermen, the spill was a financial and emotional disaster.

On a calm night the Exxon Valdez slid up on a well marked reef and sliced open her single skinned hull to release 11 million gallons of oil. Below: As was often the case, Columbia Glacier was calving huge amounts of ice directly across the tanker route. It was during evasive action to avoid the ice that the Exxon Valdez ran up on Bligh Reef.

The **Columbia Glacier**, 40 miles west of Valdez, is a big one, even by Alaska standards—some 450 square miles—and with its towering (over 200 feet high in places) six-mile-long face is as dramatic a sight as any in Alaska. It was ice from this glacier that the Exxon Valdez made its ill-fated turn to avoid.

All of Prince William Sound was hit hard by the 1964 Good Friday earthquake. In many areas the whole sea floor was lifted, destroying what had been a prosperous clam fishery. Valdez was particularly hard hit as, being built on less stable silt, it felt the violence of the quake more acutely than Whittier, just 75 miles west. Then after the shaking had essentially destroyed much of the town, four tidal waves or tsunamis demolished what was left. The damage was so bad that the town was rebuilt at a different and hopefully, more earthquake resistant site, four mile west.

Valdez—This town of some 4,000 residents, backed by high mountains, has been called Alaska's Little Switzerland.Valdez' main feature, of course is the terminal for the Alaska pipeline. It takes roughly one supertanker a day to keep up with the flow through the insulated four-foot diameter pipe that stretches 800 miles from Prudhoe Bay on the frozen Beaufort Sea.

The town has a truly spectacular setting, and is particularly popular with skiers and snowboarders seeking long runs and deep power snow. But

with no ski lift to get the customers up to the snow, local entrepreneurs have invested in helicopters to take their clients up to the mountains, at around $100 a ride. The main base for heli skiing is at Thompson Pass, about 30 miles north of town. The location is far enough away from the salt water so that the coastal weather systems affect the flying much less than if it had been based in Valdez itself.

Cordova, in the far southeast corner of Prince William Sound, is only accessed by boat and plane. Originally settled to support the copper boom in the interior to the east, Cordova has become the main fishing port of Prince William Sound, and the population almost doubles in the summer when processing workers and commercial fishermen from the lower 48 come up to fish the Copper River and work in the canneries and freezer plants.

Faced with declining salmon runs in the 1970s for pink salmon, Prince William Sound fisherman invested in a substantial hatchery program to breed and release pink salmon. The program's success went a long ways to providing a stable base for the region's fishermen.

Before the tunnel into Whittier was modified in 2000 to allow cars to drive directly through (instead of being carried on rail cars,) Prince William Sound was fairly remote. But today, because of the easier access, more and more Anchorage and lower 48 residents are discovering the charms of this sheltered archipelago.

With so many islands and sheltered waterways, Prince William Sound has become very popular with kayakers. Many outfitters offer complete trips where they supply the kayaks, gear, tents, food, etc. Then you would be dropped by boat at a remote, sheltered bay and picked up at a later date. For those seeking a bit more of an upscale experience, some outfitters travel with you, set up the tents, cook up the food and provide the entertainment.

College Fjord will be your best opportunity to see sea otters. Look particularly for what look like long dark spots on top of ice flows. Look with your binoculars—chances are they'll be sea otters, perhaps with their pups.

The hidden jewel of Prince William Sound is remote College Fjord. Within an eight-mile stretch at the upper end of this fjord five major tidewater glaciers reach the salt water. While Glacier Bay has emerged from the ice so recently that substantial trees have not gained foothold close to the ice, College Fjord is a place where the forests and glaciers have coexisted for centuries.

The result is a perspective on the great rivers of ice not seen in Glacier Bay. To see a glacier towering above the 100-foot-tall trees of a spruce forest, like **Wellesley Glacier** is really impressive.

Study the hillsides here. The upper slopes of these big glacial fjords, stripped of trees and covered with many berry bushes, are excellent bear watching territory. What you are looking for are brown or black dots that appear to be moving—these will be bears foraging for berries. Look also for white dots, often found in small groups—these will be mountain goats. You will see goats in places that an experienced rock climber would probably have trouble on.

Bears are also found down on the beach, especially if the tide is low. They are pretty good clammers, despite a crude technique. It goes like this: they look for the telltale water spurts of clams, dig them up with a big paw, smash them open with their other paw, and press the whole mass, shells and all, up to their mouth.

So where are the really big icebergs? By the time most of this ice gets to the salt water, it has been fractured so much by those twisting mountain valleys, that most of the ice that breaks off is fairly small, say the size of a small apartment building at the most.

Remember that roughly 7/8 of an iceberg is below the surface of the water, so that something that looks small on top, like the size of a garage, still poses a significant danger to ships. Small icebergs and so-called "bergy bits" are notoriously difficult to see on radar.

Calving bergs: Before Alaska cruising got so popular, few big ships penetrated right up close to the glaciers here and in other places. The captains of those ships that did discovered that if the glacier wasn't actively calving when they were there, they could often dislodge some ice with a blow of the ship's steam whistle. Today such practices are prohibited, so it's just a waiting game. Often major calving is proceeded by small bits breaking off. I was here aboard the *Dawn Princess* in 1997, and the captain spied an apartment building-sized ice spire that seemed to be tipping toward the fjord. We circled slowly for more than an hour, watching and waiting, and were finally rewarded with a splash that must have been 280 feet high and a huge boom that echoed up and down the fjord. See next pages.

Spruce forests here grow right up next to some of the glaciers, giving you a sense of scale not seen in Glacier Bay. Below: compare the photos below of the same glacier taken from almost the same spot. Top was 1997, below was 2009. The difference is very noticeable

THE 1899 HARRIMAN ALASKA EXPEDITION

Top: Seal hunter's camp with hides stretched out for drying. UW NA2103
Below: Native visitors come alongside the expedition steamer in graceful carved cedar canoes. UW NA2098

After suffering a nervous breakdown, railroad magnate (Union, Southern, and Northern Pacific) Edward H. Harriman was ordered by his doctors to have a "long vacation at sea." Prohibited from taking railroad men, he instead assembled one of the most remarkable literary, scientific, and artistic expeditions ever to come to Alaska. Chartering the steamer George W. Elder, Harriman arranged for a well-stocked library and some of the leading naturalists, artists, and scientists of the day including naturalist **John Muir**, photographer **Edward Curtis**, and many others.

Perhaps their biggest contribution was their extensive observations in Glacier Bay in June of 1899, just three months before a huge earthquake shattered many of the glaciers.

Entering Prince William Sound, they again found what some have called the two Alaskas—the spectacular beauty of the land in stark contrast to the grubbiness and even squalor of those who lived there, or like gold miners or cannery workers, exploited the resources.

Several days later, as their ship approached what

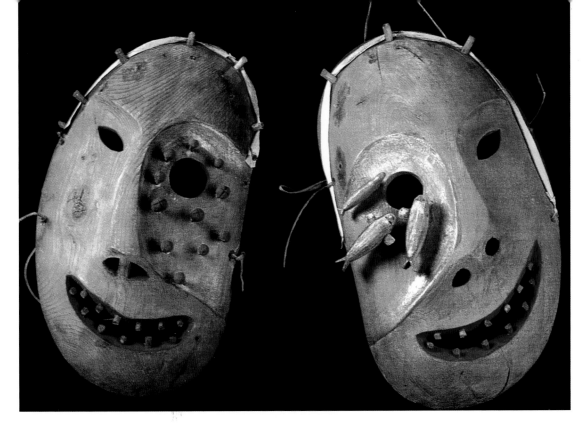

is now known as College Fjord, they made a startling discovery—while the chart showed Barry Arm ending at Barry Glacier, in fact, the glacier had receded enough for the ship to squeeze through, into the uncharted and unknown waters beyond. It was a genuine thrill for the group to discover and map this new territory that came to be named Harriman Fjord. A group including John Muir (naturally) spent two days camped in the new fjord while the ship returned to Orca for propeller repairs, after striking a rock.

Next was another unique opportunity—to name a fjord and its glaciers. Since many of his party were "Easterners," they surveyed many of the glaciers here, and named them for their New England colleges like Dartmouth, Harvard, Wellesley, and Vassar.

After leaving Prince William Sound, the George W. Elder proceeded "to the west'ard," touching at many places that are still extremely remote almost 100 years later, including King Island, Alaska, and Plover Bay, Siberia, on the Bering Strait. It was a remarkable expedition and they brought back a wealth of photographs, scientific data, and artifacts.

It's fortunate the Harriman Expedition came along when it did. For as Christian Missionaries came to Western Alaska, they viewed masks such like these as pagan and many were destroyed. ASM, IIA1451 & IIA1452 Below: Masks were mostly used by dancers in ceremonies that celebrated events in local culture. UW NA2006

Top: Leaving Whittier on the Dawn Princess in 2008. Above: when this was a big military base, these buildings wer home to about everyone in town. Bottom: take the train back to Achorage - it's way more interesting than the bus, but you'll probably need to make reservations before your cruise.

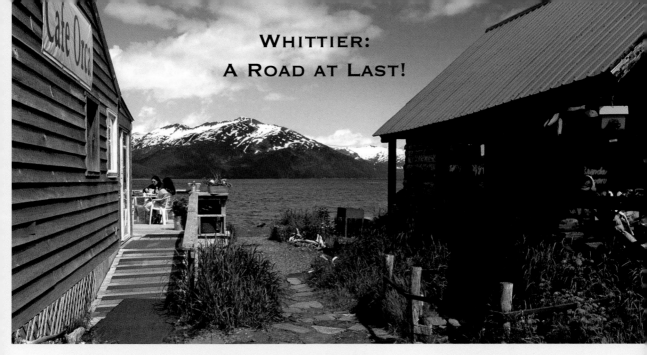

WHITTIER:
A ROAD AT LAST!

Built originally as a World War II port alternative to Seward, 1940s and 50s era residents pretty much all lived in the ugly abandoned buildings east of the docks. With heavy deep snow on the ground for most of the long winter, it was convenient to have all the homes and services, stores, movie theatre, etc. all under a single roof!

When the military pulled out in 1960, Whittier became almost a ghost town, and the 1964 earthquake almost finished off the rest.

Finally rebuilt with a larger boat harbor that gave Anchorage residents a reason to come, Whittier began to grow again. Access was still a problem—you could drive your car onto a flatbed railcar and go through the tunnel with the rest of the train, but it was hardly convenient.

Finally, in 2000, a widened tunnel was opened that accommodated both cars (one way at a time) and trains. This better access was a boost for Whittier residents, and businesses have sprung up to serve the increased numbers of visitors.

Most passengers transit Whittier quickly to and from their ship. If you do have the time, there are some modest places to shop and eat along the shore just east of the cruise ship docks. A popular whale and glacier excursion operates here as well.

Be sure to take the train in or out of Whittier instead of the bus; it's a delightful ride.

This is a place that gets a lot of snow in the winter. Most of the residents line in this high rise, where they might work and live without having to go outside.

SEWARD: NORTHERN TERMINUS

Dawn Princess at Seward. Though the big ships bring a lot of seasonal jobs to this town, commercial fishing is still a strong part of the local economy. Presently Princess ships end their Gulf of Alaska cruises in Whittier

The Good Friday Earthquake - If this town looks fairly new, it's because it is—much of the port and downtown was destroyed in the violent events of March 27, 1964. When the ground started shaking, it essentially created sort of an underwater landslide that dropped most of the waterfront six feet and into the bay. Next the big oil tanks east of town ruptured, the oil ignited in a flaming sheet across the bay and set the stage for the next tragedy: the tidal wave.

As the shaken residents began to recover from the initial shocks, few noticed that the sea had receded substantially from the shore.

Then a 30 foot wall of water, carrying much of the flaming oil with it, blasted into what was left of downtown, basically destroying the entire waterfront, and it was more than a decade before the town had rebuilt and recovered.

Today, Seward's economy runs on commercial and sport fishing as well as tourism. Look just south of the boat harbor to the parking lot usually full of trailers and motor homes—mostly Anchorage residents combining a vacation away from the bright city lights with a salmon resource. It allows them to take enough to can or freeze as a significant food resource for the winter, especially if several family members are all catching fish.

The Alaska Sealife Center, an aquarium, funded by Exxon after the oil spill, is a great place to see northern birds and mammal up close.

Seward is also the headquarters for the **Kenai Fjords National Park**, a dramatic area of narrow bays, steep islands and glaciated fjords, west of town. .

If you haven't gotten a chance to get up close to the ice yet, consider a tour or a taxi to **Exit Glacier**, about 8 miles west of town. As you'll see from the extensive glacial moraine that you will cross to get to the glacier, it is also receding at a good clip, melting away all along its front. However, be careful to give the face a respectful distance; a visitor was killed by falling ice and others have been injured.

If you're planning to spend some time in the area before heading home and have a hankering for a wilderness, but not too rough, experience, the National Park Service does maintain four remote cabins in Kenai Fjords. You'll need to bring in a sleeping bag, groceries, and maybe your fishing rod. These are fly-in; there is no road access but air taxi outfits in Seward can get you in and out. Contact the NPS at 907-224-3175 for information and availability.

Passengers that end or begin their cruise here may have a choice between train and bus to get to Anchorage. I reccomend the train; even though more expensive, it is a much more fun travel experience.

Top: Etching from Rockwell Kent's wonderful Wilderness, A Journal of Quiet Adventure in Alaska, about the winter of 1918-19, which Kent spent with his son on an island near Seward. Kent and his son were lucky to have survived all their quiet adventures! Below: Seal having fun at the Alaska Sealife Center.

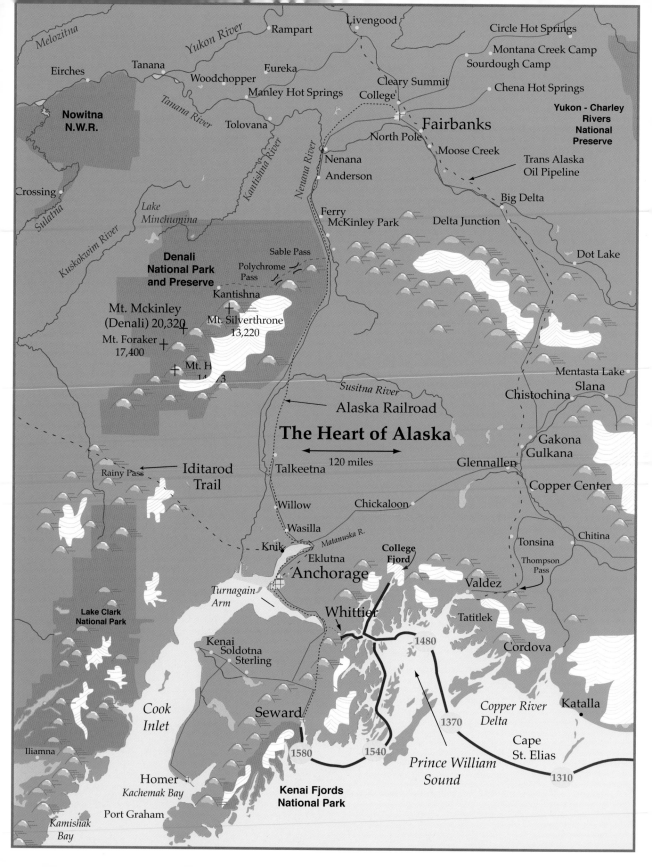

CHAPTER 8

The Heart of Alaska

Seward and Whittier to Fairbanks

"So off we went, the four dogs and I, to explore high mountains new to us.

"As the days went by, I wondered what the dogs got out of it. I had a supply of dried salmon on the sled, and they eagerly looked forward to their meal each evening. They loved to be in harness; as a matter of fact, as they were being hooked up in the morning, they were so happy that it was hard to handle them. The minute we were ready, off they would go in a great burst of speed."

— Olas J. Murie, *Journeys to the Far North*

When you plan your Alaska cruise, make time to explore a bit of the interior—at the minimum the Fairbanks-Anchorage corridor—it is so dramatically different from the coast. Cruise lines encourage people to take the Alaska Railroad. Several cruise lines have their own vista-dome style rail cars and make at least an overnight stop at Denali, and then take the paddlewheeler excursion out of Fairbanks. But if you have time, consider additional side trips.

For generations, the rivers of interior Alaska were the only highways. Paddlewheelers took freight and passengers to the most remote locations. But once the rivers froze up for the winter, travel was either by dog, horse-drawn sled, or by foot. The arrival of the first paddlewheeler in the spring with the first new food supplies and mail, was always a big event. This is the Discovery III, an excursion vessel out of Fairbanks, operated by a family that first started piloting paddle wheelers during the Yukon Gold Rush. It is a truly excellent excursion.

Top: the exquisite Russian Orthodox church at Ninilchik is built on a bluff overlooking Cook Inlet. Above: exploring in Chiswell Islands, part of the Kenai Fjords National Park, oiut of Seward,

If your cruise itinerary takes you to Seward or Whittier, consider renting a car (it may be much cheaper to travel to Anchorage first) and exploring the Kenai Peninsula, ending at **Homer**, about four and a half hours of driving. The peninsula was first settled by the Russians, and their influence is still felt, in churches, graveyards, and place names.

Ninilchik makes a great lunch stop on the way - you 'll find a small settlement overlooking Cook Inlet with an exquisite Russian Orthodox church and a number of places to eat. If you are there when the salmon are running in the Ninilchik River, you'll see what Alaskans have come to call "combat fishing," fishermen almost literally lined up bank to bank with their rods almost touching. If you haven't gotten your sportfishing fix on your cruise, this is a good place to go for salmon or halibut and there are several charter fishing operations.

Once a remote coal mining settlement, today **Homer** is a town of 5,000 set in a truly exquisite location, with a rich arts culture. Commercial fishing is the lifeblood here. Like Seward, Homer is at the very end of a road from Anchorage and is a gateway to many National and State Parks.

The Spit—Homer's most unique feature is a four-mile sand spit sticking out into Kachemak

Bay. At the end of the spit is the harbor, marine support facilities, log dump and shipping facility and a growing number of eateries, gift shops, whale watching and kayak excursions, and other businesses catering to visitors. Locals call it the Las Vegas of Alaska, but it is an integral part of the Homer experience.

Sportfishing, as you may have guessed, is excellent here. One of the local hot spots is the lagoon just north of the boat harbor—hatchery-raised fish are moved to cages in the lagoon, causing them to imprint the lagoon's location and return there as adults to try to spawn. Naturally they are a little disappointed when they get there and don't find a stream or river, just a big crowd of fishermen! At times there are so many fish here that snagging - just using bare hooks pulled through the water - is allowed.

Halibut Cove, on the opposite shore of Kachemak Bay from Homer, is a roadless fishing settlement with a strong arts flavor, and a 12 block long boardwalk. A foot ferry, the *Danny J*, offers noon departures from Homer, a stop at Gull Island, two and a half hours for exploring Halibut Cove, and a 4 P.M. return. It is a totally great day trip. Save your appetite for the Saltry Restaurant, perched on pilings above Halibut Cove with great seafood and a wonderful view.

Top: A little second home construction on Homer Spit. Above: sports fishing is huge on the Kenai Peninsula. Brenda Carney photo

ANCHORAGE - DOWNTOWN ALASKA

With the Chugach Mountains looming behind downtown and Cook Inlet in front, Anchorage has a dramatic setting. The eight-mile-long, paved Tony Knowles Coastal Trail, starting downtown, is a great walk, and an opportunity to watch shore birds. Below: Captain Cook memorial

The old saying, "You can see Alaska from here," basically describes the relationship of Anchorage and the rest of the state. While some 40% of the entire state's population resides in the greater Anchorage area, it's a good bet a lot of them blast out of town each weekend, judging from the number of planes, campers, snowmobiles, 4-wheelers, kayaks, etc., in the back yards all around town. Don't be surprised to see a moose meandering around town, though wandering bears are also regularly seen.

Though Anchorage overlooks **Cook Inlet** and **Knik Arm**, it's hardly a waterfront town in the mold of Ketchikan or Juneau. There's no place for boats to tie up downtown—the rivers draining into the inlet bring a big silt load and there are extensive tide flats making it difficult to even get to the water in most places. Most marine activity is centered in Ship Creek, north of town. Actually, most Anchorage boaters prefer to boat in Prince William Sound or the Pacific south of Seward, either trailering their boats, or keeping their boats there. Modifying the Whitter tunnel so that vehicles can just drive through - they used to have to

ride on flatcars - was a big hit with Anchorage boaters.

The newest and shiniest high-rise office buildings usually belong to Big Oil in this town. The revenue from this industry basically redefined Alaska economics, and gave its citizens the unique distinction of getting the only state dividend checks in the country. Farsighted leadership in the early days of the oil boom established a large and so far untouched "Permanent Fund" which yields enough income for checks typically in the $1,000 range annually for each of Alaska's citizens.

In recent years, North Slope oil production has fallen off, but state planners are hoping that a gas pipeline will be built to the Lower 48, creating yet another boom.

Take a few minutes and walk to the Captain Cook Memorial, overlooking the water at the end of 3rd Ave. You can get a clear sense of the very different shoreline below, but also it's an opportunity to reflect on the many unusual deeds of this English sailor, who charted much of the vast reaches of the Pacific Ocean.

Good Friday, 1964—Most folks were just settling down to supper when the most powerful earthquake to hit North America this century struck. Anchorage was mostly built on unstable clay, which is particularly susceptible to movement in an earthquake. So move it did—splitting apart, dropping whole blocks and tumbling expensive waterfront homes down

Orca mural at the old JC Penney building, downtown. Below: Downtown: the old and the new...

When the earth shook: Some sections of town were so shattered that survivors could only be reached by helicopter. UW 14501 Decorated salmon sculptures in downtown, to be auctioned off as part of a fund-raiser.

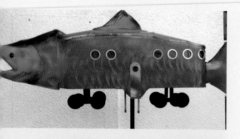

steep bluffs. Within minutes, much of the downtown core was a ruin of fallen storefronts, crumpled streets, and shattered businesses.

Property damage was extremely heavy, but fortunately only nine people died.

Shopping—if your cruise is over and you haven't done all of your shopping, it's all here in downtown. Take an evening to explore these shops and especially the galleries of native arts and crafts. There are pieces here that would be hard to find anywhere outside Alaska.

Galleries and other notable places—**Alaska Center for the Performing Arts,** 6th & F; Wolf Song of Alaska, inside J.C. Penny Mall, 6th & E; **Reeve Aviation Picture Museum**, 343 W. 6th; and **Museum of History & Art,** 121 W. 7th

---

SOME ANCHORAGE EXCURSIONS

Anchorage Flightseeing Safari
McKinley Flightseeing
Redoubt Bay Lodge Bear Viewing
Glaciers Catamaran Cruise
Glacier Discovery Train and Float Tour
Kenai Fjords National Park Cruise
Explore Anchorage City Tour

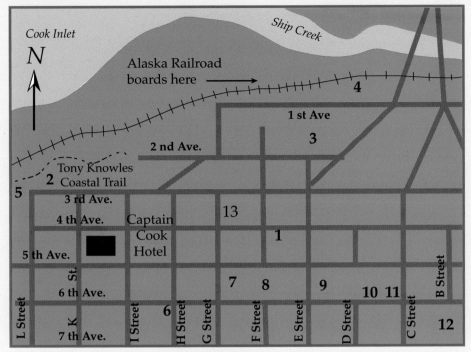

Cook Inlet

Ship Creek

N

Alaska Railroad boards here →

1 st Ave

2 nd Ave.

Tony Knowles Coastal Trail

3 rd Ave.

4 th Ave.

Captain Cook Hotel

5 th Ave.

6 th Ave.

7 th Ave.

L Street

K St.

I Street

H Street

G Street

F Street

E Street

D Street

C Street

B Street

4

3

13

1

5

2

7 8

9

10 11

6

12

Downtown Anchorage

1. Log Cabin and Visitor Information Center
2. Tony Knowles Coastal Trail - ten mile trail that follows the shore with great views.
3. Alaska Statehood Monument
4. Alaska Railroad Depot
5. Resolution Park with Captain Cook Monument
6. Oomingmak Musk-ox Producers Co-Op— unique garments from strange creatures.
7. Alaska Center for the Performing Arts
8. Town Square Municipal Park
9. Reeve Aviation Picture Museum
10. Alaska State Trooper Museum
11. Wolf Song of Alaska - large wolf exhibit.
12. Anchorage Museum of History and Art— excellent collection; gift shop and cafe.
13. Alaska Public Lands Information Center

Right: Contemporary Eskimo visor at the Anchorage airport.

THE ALASKA RAILROAD

In the stillness of a September morning, dome cars wait for their northbound travelers. Below: Winding along the Susitna River Canyon. It was near here that pilot extraordinaire Don Sheldon landed his floatplane in a rescue mission that became legend. See story on following pages.

"**Anchorage, September 14, 1997, 7:45 A.M.:** Our train sits waiting on a siding, near the water. The other passengers board quickly, their breath white in the chill morning air, but I stand aside, let the bus leave, to take in the surroundings. The days get shorter quickly in the fall this far north and the sun is still behind the Chugach Mountains to the east, yet just illuminating the volcanoes along the snowy wall of the Alaska Range, across Cook Inlet. The shiny sides of the coaches are yellow and pink, reflecting the sky, while all around is almost dark. Here and there along the waiting train, steamy air vents from beneath the coaches, cloak all in a mysterious other-world feeling. The last whistle finally blows, and I have to board. Yet I linger until the very last, unwilling to leave the drama of this moment."

Until 1972, when the George Parks Highway north to Fairbanks was completed, the train was the only transportation there was for the folks along much of the Anchorage - Fairbanks corridor.

Whistle stops were an everyday part of train life as the "local" trains dropped homesteaders off

with their bags and boxes of groceries and supplies, often at trail heads where horses or four-wheel-drive vehicles waited to take them down some lonely dirt track to a remote home. Since the Highway was completed, winter passenger service is limited to weekends and Thursdays

Every spring the passenger specials begin, with the domed cars that make it one of the most scenic rail rides in North America. Each day there is a northbound and a southbound passenger run. These trains generally have three different kinds of domed cars. Several cruise lines have had special railcars constructed for their passengers. These dome cars are usually a modification of dome cars used by railroads in the US western states. The domed section is usually made longer along with other improvements including gift shops and other passenger amenities.

However you travel, these dome cars provide a wonderful chance to experience this dramatic country. Especially early and late in the season, you see some of the thousands, perhaps even millions, of birds and waterfowl travel each spring and fall in their annual migrations.

Some of these birds, like the Arctic Tern - See P 260 - make truly stunning migrations. Plus the number of birds involved in these annual migrations runs into the millions.

Crossing the Nenana River: it's mid-September and the leaves are flying! These rebuilt vistadome style cars, operated by several cruise lines, offer excellent viewing upstairs and elegant dining downstairs. Below: Some cars offer special areas for photographers, like this covered rear platform.

Truly remarkable travelers, the Arctic Tern (black cap, red bill and feet, with a long, forked tail) summers in Alaska then takes off each fall for a 10,000 mile journey to winter in the Antarctic (it's summer there). Look for them in the Knik marshes.

Good soil and long hours of daylight in summer makes for some very large vegetables, like this cabbage near Fairbanks.

"Fer Cris'sake, all it would take is for one of those Alaska Airlines jets to cream into Mt. Juneau and it'd take the the whole legislature with it..."
— Heard around Alaska

Now that you've taken the cruise, seen Southeast Alaska and steamed up the wild and lonely coast to Seward, doesn't it seem a bit like there are two Alaskas? The drizzly, grey one down there with Ketchikan and Juneau, and the wide open one up here with Anchorage, Fairbanks and the whole really, really, big rest of the state? And doesn't it seem odd that the capital, Juneau, is so isolated down there? This same thought has occurred to many Alaskans. In the 1970s when the state was flush with oil revenues, "Move The Capital" was a popular bumper sticker

The only problem was where to move it. Anchorage and Fairbanks were such rivals that neither would accept the other as capital. So why not pick some centrally located spot in between, and make that the capital? Brilliant! So, in 1976, Alaskans voted to build a new capital near Willow, mile 185.7. So where is it, you say? Cooler heads prevailed when the first cost estimates came out...

Now and again, through the trees, you'll glimpse a road, the George Parks Highway, just to the west, or left of the train. Between this highway and the Bering Sea coast, 500 miles to the west, there are no roads. (Well, O.K., there are a few exceptions—the 20 miles of bumpy pavement between Naknek and King Salmon, on Bristol Bay, a few miles around Dillingham and a few more around Nome.)

The forest here is known as taiga, very different from that of Prince William Sound and Southeast Alaska. Gone are the tall hemlocks and cedars, replaced by low white and black spruce, poplar, birch, aspen and larch. Where the trees seem particularly stunted is a sign of either wet muskeg or frozen permafrost close to the surface.

Sometimes the train slows near mile 224, to let travelers get a good view of the Alaska range : Denali at 20,320', and her lower sisters, Mt. Hunter, 14,573', and Mt. Foraker, 17,400'.

The Susitna River is normally placid, but about 65 miles northeast of here the turns violent in a five-mile rapids named Devil's Canyon.

Talkeetna pilot Don Sheldon saw the wreckage of a U.S. Army survey boat in the canyon on a charter flight to a nearby lake, and upon returning, spotted survivors huddling on the rocky shore with almost no way out, unless he could somehow land in the river canyon. The rapids in the river created 6-foot waves—certain death to land on, but after a couple of passes through, Sheldon found a little strip of calmer water, where he thought it might just be possible to land. Sheldon made his approach, swallowed hard, and set his little Aeronica down. Once he was in the water, he had to let it carry him backwards, into the rapids, for him to get to the survivors were:

"As the plane backed into the first of the combers, I felt it lurch heavily fore and aft. It was like a damned roller coaster. The water was rolling up higher than my wingtips, beating at the struts, and I could barely see because of the spray and water on the windows. All of a sudden the engine began to sputter and choke, and I knew it was getting wet down pretty good..."
—Don Sheldon, in *Wager With the Wind,*

Somehow the engine kept going, and Sheldon managed to maneuver close enough to shore for one of the men to clamber aboard. Getting out was almost as hard—backing the plane down the rapids, until he came to another stretch just barely long enough to effect a take-off. Sheldon had to repeat this remarkable performance three more times to get all the survivors out.

Look for the little airstrip, through the trees to the east at Talkeetna. This village is the staging area for almost all expeditions to the top of Denali, and for most it begins with a flight to Kahiltna Glacier.

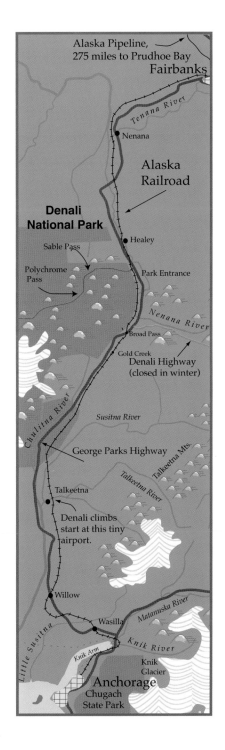

DENALI

Consider yourself lucky if you get a view like this one from a hill above the Mt. McKinley Princess Wilderness Lodge. That's Denali in the center and 17,400' Mt. Foraker on the left. The Alaska Range essentially forms a barrier between two very different weather systems and climates. The result is that the mountain, unfortunately, is often covered by clouds. Early climbers had to struggle through the lowland forest and rugged lower slopes of the range before the hard part of their climb even began. Today ski-equipped small planes take climbing parties up to the new starting place at about 7,000 feet up.

Early explorers sometimes got a glimpse of a very high mountain to the north of Cook Inlet, a peak the natives of the region called Denali, which meant "The High One." An early prospector named it Mt. McKinley, but most Alaskans today refer to it as simply Denali.

At 20,320 feet, it is the tallest peak in North America. If this mountain were in California, or perhaps Peru, it would be a world class climb, but it wouldn't have the particular challenges that come with its high latitude.

The Alaska Range is a wall between Yukon - Arctic highs and North Pacific lows. The result is a highly volatile microclimate, and a mountain that can basically create its own weather very rapidly. Most climbing fatalities here are caused by rapid weather changes, combining wind, cold, and snow.

Many climbing parties have had the bitter experience of being turned back, sometimes just a few hundred yards short of the summit by wind and cold. Experienced Denali climbers know that they can only get near the top and hope that the mountain gods will allow them to tread on the top of the continent.

An Imposter's Claim—One of the oddest episodes in Denali's history was the 1906 claim by Dr. Frederick Cook, a very experienced Arctic explorer, that he and a companion had made it to the top of the mountain, the first to do so, bringing

down photographs for proof. Climbers familiar with the mountain doubted Cook's claims, but it wasn't until 1910 that a group, specifically climbing to dispute Cook, found the supposed summit photographed by Cook: 10,000 feet lower and 20 miles away from the actual summit.

Denali Today—The mountain has become a very popular climb, sought each summer by expeditions from all over the world.

However today's climbers face a much easier prospect than the early climbers. Instead of starting on the ground near Talkeetna, and struggling for several days before they even got to the top of the first glacier, they hop a plane from the Talkeetna airstrip and get dropped off at the base camp at Kahiltna Glacier at 7,000 feet. In a typical summer literally hundreds of climbers try to find a break in the weather and make it to the top so, this base camp is a busy place, with a ranger station, aircraft, and climbing parties coming and going. How very, very different from the rigors faced by the mountain's true pioneers!

But Denali should never be taken for granted. It remains an extremely challenging ascent, as witnessed by regular fatalities among those who attempt it.

Opposite: On Denali, 1932. When we look at all the high tech equipment today's climbers consider essential, our respect for the feats of the pioneer climbers grows. And especially since those climbers had to do without the services of pilots like Don Sheldon who with ski-equipped aircraft would drop them on Kahiltna Glacier, 7,000 feet up, saving today's climbers weeks of hiking with all their heavy gear! UAF Rasmuson Library 81-218-07n

"...The storm now became so severe that I was actually afraid to get new dry mittens out of my rucksack, for I knew my hands would be frozen in the process... The last period of our climb is like the memory of an evil dream. La Voy was completely lost in the ice mist, and Professor Parker's frosted form was an indistinct blur above me... The breath was driven from my body and I held to my axe with stooped shoulders to stand against the gale; I couldn't go ahead. As I brushed the frost from my glasses and squinted upward through the stinging snow, I saw a sight that will haunt me to my dying day. The slope above me was no longer steep! That was all I could see. What it meant I will never know for certain—all I can say is that we were close to the top."

— Belmore Browne, *The Conquest of Mt. McKinley*

"I was snowshoeing along about fifty feet back of the sled, with Harry (Liek) right behind me when, without warning, the snow fell away under my snowshoes. I plunged into sudden darkness.

I had time to let out a feeble shout. Then for a couple of long, long seconds I plummeted downward. I remember thinking, 'This is it, fellow!' Then my pack scraped against the slide of the crevasse, my head banged hard against the ice wall and I came to a jarring stop.

When my head cleared and I could look around in the blue darkness, I saw I was on a plug of snow wedged between the ice walls. On either side, this wedge of snow fell away into sheer blackness.

About forty feet above me I could see a ray of sunlight, slanting through the hole I had made in the surface crust. The crevasse was about twelve feet wide up there, it narrowed to two feet down where I was. Below was icy death."

— Grant Pearson, *My Life of High Adventure*

"But in half an hour, we stood on the narrow edge of the spur top, facing failure. Here, where the black ridge leading to the tops of the pink cliffs should have flattened, all was absolutely sheer, and a hanging glacier, bearded and dripping with bergschrunds, filled the angle in between...I heard Fred say, 'It ain't that we can't find a way that's possible, taking chances. There ain't *no* way.'

"We were checkmated with steepness, at 11,300 feet with eight days of mountain food on our hands. But remember this: also with scarce two weeks provisions below with which to reach the coast and winter coming. The foolishness of the situation, and the fascination, lies in the fact that except in this fair weather, unknown in Alaska at this season, we might have perished either night in those two exposed camps."

— Robert Dunn, *Shameless Diary of an Explorer*

"We tried to take some snaps, but had to give it up. For four minutes only did I leave my mittens off, and in that time, I froze five tips of my fingers to such a degree that after they had first been white, some weeks later, they turned black, and at last fell off, with the nails and all.."

— Erling Strom, *How We Climbed Mt. McKinley*

"There was no pride of conquest, no trace of that exultation of victory some enjoy over the first ascent of a lofty peak, no gloating over good fortune that had hoisted us a few hundred feet higher than others who had struggled and been discomfited. Rather...that a privileged communion with the high places of the earth had been granted... secret and solitary since the world began. All the way down, unconscious of weariness in the descent, my thoughts were occupied with the glorious scene my eyes gazed upon, and should gaze upon never again."

— Hudson Stuck, in *Mt. McKinley:*
The Pioneer Climbs by Terris Moore

Above: Climber Belmore Brown made three Denali attempts, but was defeated each time. ASL PCA 01-3441

"... My mind was racing. I had to grab the rock near Dave with my left hand; it was bare, no mitten or sock. It would be frozen. I had to. Suddenly my bare hand shot out to grab the rock. Slicing cold.

I saw Dave's face, the end of his nose raw, frostbitten. His mouth, distorted into an agonized mixture of compassion and anger, swore at me to get a glove on. I looked at my hand. It was white, frozen absolutely white."

– Art Davidson, *Minus 148 Degrees, The*
Winter Ascent of Mt. McKinley

RULES FOR BEAR COUNTRY

Brown, or grizzly (or just 'griz'), as well as black bear are common throughout this part of Alaska. While for the most part bears are content to mind their own business, visitors should remember a few rules.

First, let bears know you're around by talking, singing, wearing bells, etc. when you hike though the woods or wherever visibility is reduced. If a bear knows you're coming, he'll probably want to get out of your way. If, however, you surprise one on a narrow trail, it could get ugly, for you. Bears react badly to surprise...

Don't get between a mother and her cubs, or a bear and its food. Sometimes people have been mauled when they inadvertently got between a mother and cub, without knowing it, in thick bushes. If you see a bear, assume there are cubs nearby.

Don't run It could trigger an automatic, "chase food" reaction. Bears may look big and lumbering, but when they want to do so, they can accelerate faster than a man ever could.

Be careful where you put your food. Problems have sometimes arisen from campers carelessly leaving food out or stored near or in their tent or vehicle. Put your food in a container, away from your tent.

Bear encounter: the makings of a dangerous situation. In this case, we were walking down the road when there was a rustling in the bushes and two bear cubs appeared. At 200 pounds, cuddly they were not. We were taken aback and essentially stopped in our tracks, the bears 50 feet or so ahead. Then the mom appeared, about the size of a Volkswagon, and definitely alarmed about seeing us so close to her cubs. Without turning around and actually running, which could have triggered the 'chase food' reaction, we walked backwards about as fast as we could. My 14-year old son, who was with us, forgot everything we had told him and just started running. When I finally caught up with him later, I told him he'd just flunked the bear test!

DENALI NATIONAL PARK

Denali watching at the Eielson Visitors Center, about a three hour bus ride from the main visitors center by the park entrance. Alaskastock The weather isn't always just like this... Below: bear protective equipment is a growth industry here...

The park was originally established in 1917 as Mt. McKinley National Park, a wildlife preserve that didn't include the mountain for which it is named. Finally in 1980, the protected area was tripled in size, to include the entire mountain massif along with caribou herd winter range and calving grounds and renamed Denali National Park and Preserve.

The park has become sort of an icon for vistors, representing all that they have come to Alaska for. Yet, some, especially those who just have time for an overnight or two at Glitter Gulch –the nickname for the lodges/shops area just outside the park entrance–come away disappointed. Hours of bus riding on bumpy, dusty roads, a bear or moose sighting, maybe a glimpse of Denali through the clouds, didn't match up to the advertisements.

A bit of advice: the park's true grandeur lies in its being, as much as is possible with the limited visitor access, an intact subarctic ecosystem. For many, Denali Park is experienced in a bus with a naturalist/driver. For others, a visit might include camping at Wonder Lake, with backpacking through the wilderness. Don't expect a park with the visitor facilities of Yellowstone or the Grand Canyon.

Glimpsing Denali: If you get a view of the mountain that looks anything like the photos in

this chapter, consider yourself very lucky. Denali is so high that it acts as a mixing area for weather from the Gulf of Alaska and the great interior, meaning a lot of cloudy days. Generally in summer, expect two days out of three to be overcast. In reality your best views from the mountain are apt to be from the Georges Park Highway, or from the Alaska Railroad, or from a place like the Mt. McKinley Princess Wilderness Lodge, near Talkeetna.

Take a walk: there are some good trails, like the Horseshoe Lake Trail, near the lodges at Glitter Gulch, so get out there! This is bear country, so while you don't need to be terrified, making noise is good. Remember, in almost all cases, if bears can hear you, they will get out of the way.

Getting around: Private vehicles are only allowed as far as the Savage River checkpoint, about 14 miles in. Shuttle buses: The ARA Courtesy Shuttle, a beige bus loops between Glitter Gulch, the park visitor center, and Mckinley Village; schedules in hotels. The Sled Dog Demonstration Shuttle loops between the visitor center, Riley Creek campground and the Park Headquarters in time for the sled dog demonstrations at 10, 2, &4. The Park Shuttle–green bus– is the main way of getting into the interior of the park, leaving the visitor center every hour for Wonder Lake (5.5 hr. one way $31 RT) and on the half hour to Eielson (4hr. one way $22.50 RT). Wildlife is often best viewed early, so consider getting up and onto one of the early buses. Wonder Lake is a spectacular place and the site for many of the photos of Denali, but 8 or 10 hours of bus riding is a lot. Your chances of seeing wildlife from a bus are high, and generally unless the animals are so close as to possibly pose a danger, buses will stop and allow passengers out for a photo opportunity.

---- Traveler Tip ----

There are no food, drinks, meals, film, insect repellent, etc. available in the park (except at Kantishna, 90 miles in...) even at the visitor's center, so bring what you need with you on the bus. This is not like the lower 48 National Parks with their many vendors, restaurants, etc.

In the bus, Denali National Park, Sept 17, 1997: We didn't have to wait very long to see wildlife; just five minutes after entering the park, we stopped to watch two very big, brown, and somewhat disheveled-looking moose wandering through the low bushes perhaps 25 yards from the bus. Big is the operative word here. Everyone is concerned about bears, but I wouldn't want to meet a moose face-to-face on a narrow trail either.

A little later our sharp-eyed driver pulled over again and directed our attention to a place on the hillside where something brown could be seen moving. This was nature in the raw—you needed binoculars to see it. A big 'griz' was chowing down on what looked like a side of Dall sheep. "

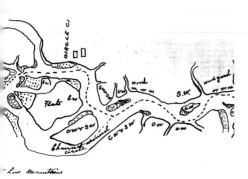

Yukon sketch charts were often hand drawn and passed from skipper to skipper.

The big weird thing near mile 362, as the train emerges from the Nenana River canyon is the Usibelli coal tipple. Inside is the equipment for filling the coal cars that run north to Fairbanks, or all the way south to Seward to be loaded aboard ships for the Orient.

The country changes substantially here as the trees seem to swallow us up until it seems we're traveling in a leafy canyon. This is all the northern tiaga—a taste of the vast, low, mixed black spruce and birch forests that cover much of the Yukon basin that drains interior Alaska. Plants and trees don't get very big here; the growing season is short and the ground has great frozen areas (permafrost) just below the surface.

The country is so flat here that the Nenana, barely thirty yards wide in places in the gorge, and rushing along faster than a man can run, breaks into many branches like Seventeenmile and Lost Slough, and almost seems to just disappear into the flats before finally rejoining to enter the Tanana River at Nenana. Early travelers on rafts often had to pole tediously through miles of shallows here.

Look for the big black and white wooden tripod (about 30' high), between the tracks and the river at Nenana, **mile 411.** Each winter this tower is dragged out onto the frozen river for the Nenana Ice Classic, a uniquely Alaskan lottery. What folks bet on is "Ice Out," the moment in spring when the frozen river breaks up.

It's entirely fitting that this be celebrated, for the rivers are the lifeblood for most of the towns in the immense drainage of the Yukon River.

Where there are no highways, the arrival of the first freight barge in the spring is always an exciting community event. This freight (usually in 40' containers or vans) usually begins its water journey from Seattle, stacked five and six high on a huge 400' oceangoing barge, towed by a 5,000 horsepower tug. Somewhere near the mouth of the Yukon River, perhaps at St. Michaels, the containers would be hoisted onto a smaller barge, to be pushed upstream. Sometimes, for freight bound for communities on the smaller rivers, the container would be transferred a third time, onto a yet smaller barge, pushed by an even smaller tug.

The River Country

Navigation is still tough! The river channels sometimes shift every few weeks; there are few buoys or navigational aids. Captains use hand drawn charts passed along from other captains and pilots. Sometimes the only way through is launching a skiff to sound out a particularly tricky channel before you entered it. Even with all these precautions, groundings are routine.

The river as highway. Despite what you may hear, not everyone who lives out in the bush has a floatplane in their backyard. But the majority of villages and settlements in the vast country between the Alaska Range and the Bering Sea and Arctic Ocean lie along one of the many rivers with native and Russian names like Kitchatna, Tonzona, Kantishna, Hoholitna, and Chilikadrotna, Ugashik, Nushagak, and Kinak. When the ice is out, watercraft ranging from big tugs and barges to outboard jet boats move people and supplies around. When the ice is in, it is usually hard and smooth enough for vehicles.

It was during those in-between months, the short spring and falls, that travel was difficult. **Suddenly, around mile 466, Civilization appears**—houses, streets, and people mowing lawns. After what seems like the endless tiaga forest stretching unbroken to the horizon, coming upon civilization so suddenly is almost a shock. First is College, and the University of Alaska at **mile 467**, and then a few miles later, Fairbanks.

Top: Oops, this paddlewheeler stayed on the upper Yukon a little too late, and is about to get frozen in for the winter. Its passengers might have a long hard hike ahead of them. Yukon archives. Above: how the wealthy traveled to the Gold Rush - Paddlewheeler White Horse in Five Finger Rapids, Yukon RIver. UW 21255

Take the time to read the bronze plaques beneath the Pioneer's Memorial in downtown Fairbanks. It's a moving tribute to the courage and perseverance of the early settlers. The winters here are considerably colder than at Anchorage and the days noticeably longer in summer and shorter in winter. Imagine what it must have been like before electricity, indoor plumbing and central heating! Opposite page: Floatplanes along the shore of the Tanana River.

The Wandering Trader—In the summer of 1901, E.T. Barnette was headed for the upper Tanana with a load of trading goods. Shallow water forced him to unload his goods right in front of what is now the Fairbanks Visitor's Bureau log cabin. He started to build an even shallower-draft vessel to keep going up the river, but when gold was discovered nearby, Barnette decided to build his trading post right where he was and Fairbanks was born.

Fairbanks today has a more stable economy, with a large military contingent from nearby Fort Wainwright and Eielson Air Force Base. For much of the century, however, it went through the many boom and busts that characterize so much of Alaskan economy.

> "Thirty below zero this morning. Frost has crept through the walls and caused the bedclothes to stick to the wall on that side and it is mortal agony to crawl out of the warm nest in the center of the bed when daddy called."
> — Margaret Murie, *Two in The Far North*

Winter in Fairbanks lasts from October to April, and before the modern conveniences like plumbing, electricity and oil heat, these months were an unrelenting challenge for residents, especially for women, perhaps raising families with their men away. Margaret Murie, who came to Fairbanks in 1911 when she was nine, grew up with a keen memory of the routines and community activities that made life manageable for the women of Fairbanks.

The river was the highway, and the nearest town was ten days away by river boat. Between freeze-up in the fall and ice out in the spring, there was only the weekly horse-drawn mail sleigh that traveled a difficult trail through the mountains and over the frozen rivers to Valdez.

Ice out was a big event—notices were posted around town to keep residents informed: "Ice moved at Fort Gibbon this morning at 8 a.m.," for the first steamer of the season meant fresh vegetables, followed shortly thereafter by the "slaughterhouse boat" with its pens of cows, sheep, pigs, geese, and chickens, brought up from Seattle.

In a town of log homes that heated with wood, fire was always a worry. A big steam pump at the Northern Commercial Company power plant was always ready to pump river water from under the river ice to fight fires. On at least one occasion, when the wood-fired boilers couldn't keep up with the demands of a big fire, the cry went out to "Bring the bacon"—case after case of oily bacon was brought from the warehouse, thrown into the boilers, the steam pressure rose, the water flowed once more, and the fire was contained.

Today Fairbanks is the most northerly city in North America. There are many of the conveniences found elsewhere, but the long winters are still bitter, bitter cold, with all their unique problems like having your car go bumpity bump in the mornings because of the frozen flat place in the tires from sitting on the street all night long.

Top: The Trans Alaska Pipeline is a major visitor attraction and is included in some Faribanks excursions. Above: float planes on the Chena River. A bush pilot demonstrating short field landings is often included in a riverboat trip.

273

The most popular tour in Fairbanks is aboard this paddle-wheeler, whose owners have been operating paddlewheelers on the rivers of Alaska for several generations. The Discovery makes a stop in front of the river-front homestead of the late Ididarod racer, Susan Butcher, where her busband, David Monson, or another dog handler will introduce their puppies. Another stop will be at an Athabascan village, where natives share their culture and crafts. A popular tour is a combination of the Riverboat Discovery, a Gold Mine vist, and a stop at the Trans Alaska Oil Pipeline.

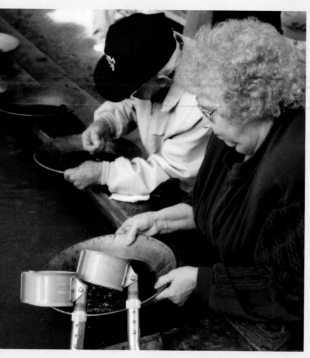

Aboard the Riverboat
DISCOVERY

Tales from 'Westward'
(Western Alaska)

Top: Airport at the remote settlement at Coffee Point, on the Egegik River. Above: graveyard, South Naknek. Russian influence is still very stong in western Alaska.

This isn't your regular Alaska - the vastness of this coast is hard to grasp. From the border with Russia in the far west of the Aleutian Islands to Bering Strait in the north, the Bering Sea washes a coast longer than the distance from Maine to Florida.

The land is treeless and austere, the settlements few and remote, rarely connected to each other and none to the 'outside' by roads.

The climate is dramatically harsher than that of Southeast Alaska. There is no gentle and sheltering forest, no warm offshore current to temper the extremes of weather. In the native communities of southern Alaska winter was often a time for crafts, for family, an often welcome change from the busy pace of salmon fishing and berry gathering that characterized the summers. But along much of the mainland Bering Sea coast, before the white man's processed food was available, winter could be another word for starvation. The sea along the shore froze, game was scarce. Family survival depended on the success of the man, the hunter.

And far more than in any other part of coastal Alaska, the settlements of this coast are predominantly native Alaskans: Aleuts along the Aleutian Islands, Yup'ik Eskimos from Bristol Bay to Norton Sound and Inupiat Eskimos from there north.

All had evolved from tribes who migrated from Siberia over a land bridge across Bering Strait during an ice age some 30,000 years ago. Once across, they evolved into several native groups, each with its own language.

The Great King Crab Fishery

In the early 1960s Alaskan fishermen began to expand fishing for a remarkable spider-like creature—the king crab. Unlike most crab, king crab traveled in herds across the bottom of the Bering Sea. When fishing was good, the big pots would come up with up to 2,000 pounds of crab after less than 24 hours in the water. Boats would get a 200,000-pound load in 48 hours! It was legendary money, but legendary work as well—when you were on the crab, 18 - 20 hours on deck a day were routine.

The heaviest concentration of crab was found in the Alaska Peninsula - Bering Sea - Aleutian Islands area. In the winter, this area has some of the stormiest weather in the world, and many able vessels and crews were lost to violent winds, big seas, and low temperatures. Perhaps the biggest threat was the buildup of heavy ice on a vessel's superstructure and any crab pots on deck when below freezing temperatures combined with strong winds, a fairly regular event.

After almost two decades of spectacular growth both in catch and fleet size, the crab population crashed in the early 1980's. For a while the joke in Alaska banks was that when you started a new account, you got a crab boat free as a premium.

Today the crab fishery continues, but at a much lower harvest level than in the boom days of the '70s and early '80s. In recent years the TV show, "The Deadliest Catch" celebrates the fishery and its risks.

Top: Crewman Walter Kuhr aboard the king crabber Flood Tide, Bering Sea, 1971. During the 1970s, there were so many crab that when the holds were full, the crew would keep fishing, just putting the crab on deck. Then they would anchor, and lower the level of the circulating sea water in the holds, and cram in the rest of the crab! Even crowded, the crab could survive the 12-18 hour run in to unload. Above: The Bering Sea is always probing, always trying to find a vessel's weak spot. Here the almost brand new Key West sinks after a crab pot broke loose from its lashings during a storm, and broke off a 12" diameter vent pipe, flooding the lazarette and sinking the boat. As you can see, another boat was nearby and picked up the crew. Bart Eaton photo.

Top: Six American whalers anchored at Port Clarence, AK, with Eskimo tents on shore, circa 1900. Tent on left has carved ivory figures on a pole. Occasionally whalers would spend the winter far to the east, in the protected harbor at Herschel Island, in order to be able to persue whales in the spring. This is one of my favorite Alaska pictures. UW NA2125

Right, landing party at Bogoslov Island, Bering Sea, circa 1905. These men were lucky - a US Navy ship was about to drop them to explore the newly formed island when it got an emergency radio call to another island, so they couldn't get ashore. When they returned a few weeks later, instead of an island they found a column of smoke and ash blowing two miles up into the sky! UW Nowell 5718

Cap Thomsen
and the Aleutian Mailboat

"Cap" Thomsen aboard the iced-up Expansion after a difficult trip up Shelikof Strait to Seward in winter-time. Top: Is this a boat? The Expansion iced up at Seward. Icing up was a constant problem for vessels traveling the western Alaska coast in winter. Photos courtesy Niels Thomsen

In the 1950s, the only outside contact for 19 isolated native villages on the Alaska Peninsula and Aleutian Islands was the 114-foot mailboat *Expansion*, which made regular round trips from Seward, skippered by owner Niels "Cap" Thomsen, one of those entrepreneurs that Alaska seems to attract. About the first thing "Cap" noticed on his stops was how some native villages seemed to have a lot of single young men, and another village, maybe a hundred miles away, single women, but neither group of singles was aware of the others:

"So I bought a Polaroid camera and took pictures of the unmarried natives. I'd write their names and towns on them: 'Nona Popalook from Gambrel Bay,' etc. I put the pictures up on two bulletin boards, one for single women and another for single men. Pretty soon after that the word was out, and any time we'd round a point to come into a harbor where a native village was, the singles would be jumping into their boats and rowing out as fast as they could to meet us even before we got the anchor down! They'd come aboard and head right for the singles bulletin boards. Also back in those days, to be legally married, the natives had to go to Cold Bay, a long way away. So I got a Justice of the Peace license, so I could marry them right aboard the boat!"

— "Cap" Niels Peter Thomsen

"Cap," also advertised his summer mailboat trips for birdatchers, but his brochure might have added in the section describing the visit to Dutch Harbor, "And help your captain paint his other boat," For "Cap" had purchased a tired processor ship, and tried to work on it for a few days whenever he was in Dutch.

Top right: Ken Lisburn watercolor of a traditional summer camp where Eskimo families, go to catch and dry fish for winter. Author's collection. Opposite middle: King Island ivory carvers on the beach at Nome, circa 1920. The long white object is a cribbage board being carved out of a walrus tusk. UW17963. Opposite lower: Eskimo group with fish drying on racks, Cape Prince of Wales around 1915. UW17964. Above: Shopping, Eskimo style, circa 1910. This group is aboard one of the several trading schooners that traveled from Seattle to the Arctic each summer to trade food and supplies for ivory and furs. UW 1762 Right: A Shaman in a mask and carved hands tries to exorcise evil spirits from a sick child. Shamans were unable to cure diseases, especially smallpox, that the early whalers and traders brought with them and lost much face in their communities. UW Thwaites 0134-493

INUPIAT
Glimpses of an Eskimo Past

Scattered along the northern and western coasts are the Eskimo communities. Traditionally dependent on seals, whales, and caribou, this was a culture where winter was another word for hunger.

Today's eskimos are more apt to live in prefab houses, delivered by the annual barge, and depend on seasonal fishing and construction work. Unfortunately, alcoholism and drug use is a continual problem in the remote native villages.

One of the bigger problems facing the remote villages is the effects of global warming. Almost all are built close to the water. Rising sea levels combined with the lack of protection that sea ice afforded from heavy seas, means that coastal erosion claims more land each year.

Additionally, permafrost, ice close to the surface, underlies most of these villages, and as it melts, buildings require substantial work to keep them from sinking into the tundra.

GLOBAL WARMING:

As the ice disappears...

"It's completely beyond what any of our models had predicted." "I never expected it to melt this fast." Such were the comments among scientists at a recent symposium on the Arctic. There still may be debate in a few quarters about global warming, but not in Arctic Alaska: it's here.

The tidewater glaciers up and down the Alaska coast had been receding slowly for years even before global warming was a household word. But recent events in the Arctic and implications for the future, especially for species dependent on wide areas of sea ice like the polar bear, are sobering.

Up until a decade or so ago, the sea ice covered most of the Arctic in winter, melting and receding a bit in the summer and then refreezing again in the winter. But in recent years the sea ice has receded dramatically in the summer. From 1979-2000, the average area of ice in the Arctic was around three million square miles. In August of 2007, that number had shrunk by half, a truly staggering reduction. One scientist predicted that the Arctic would be totally ice free in summer by 2030!

It may even happen sooner, for as the ice melts, the darker ocean absorbs much more heat than the white ice which reflects the sun's rays, further increasing the melting.

In the changes this brings there would be losers and winners. The Northwest Passage ship route from Atlantic to Pacific would become reality. Vast new areas would be open for mineral and oil exploration. Valuable fish species like salmon and pollock might thrive and move their range further north.

The polar bear would probably be a loser. They depend on the ice pack for habitat and if it disappeared in the summer, the only polar bears would be in zoos.

Many native villages in the Arctic are built close to the shore, but had been protected from storm seas by the ice. As the ice recedes, the seas become larger, and villages must either relocate or eventually be swept away. Permafrost–frozen earth close to the surface of the ground–is another huge issue. Most small buildings and houses in the Arctic essentially have permafrost foundations. As the ice in soil melts, the buildings slowly settle into the soggy ground.

Can global warming be stopped? In theory, yes. But the realities of a rapidly developing Asia and a global economy built on high energy use make it unlikely.

So–if you want to see Alaska in its present state, go soon!

Acknowledgments

I am indebted to a number of unusually talented people, without whom this book would have been far less than what it is.

In particular to my designer, Martha Brouwer, of Waterfront Press, for her skill and grace in taking a sheaf of text, maps and drawings and fashioning them page by page into art.

To my old pen pals, John and Peggy Hanson, for their ideas, and valuable suggestions.

To John J. O'Ryan, for allowing me to quote freely from his unusual book, *The Maggie Murphy.*

To John Pappenheimer, of Waterfront Press, for his continual support, excitement, and direction.

To my family, for encouraging me through a long project.

To many friends and shipmates, in all manner of craft, in many a breezy cove and strait, for sharing so many stories of the coast.

And finally to old Mickey Hansen, passed away but not forgotten, for his kindness in taking a greenhorn kid under his wing aboard the old *Sydney,* in 1965, showing him the way of a ship and the true magic of The North.

Bibliography

Allen, Arthur, *A Whaler & Trader in the Arctic*. Anchorage: Alaska Northwest Books,1978.

Armstrong, Robert H. *A Guide to the Birds of Alaska*, Seattle: Alaska Northwest Books, 1991.

Blanchet, M. Wylie. *The Curve of Time*, N. Vancouver: Whitecap Books Ltd., 1990.

Bohn, Dave. *Glacier Bay: The Land and the Silence*. New York: Ballantine Books, 1967.

Bolotin, Norm. *Klondike Lost*. Anchorage: Alaska Northwest Publishing, 1980.

Caldwell, Francis, *Land of the Ocean Mists*, Seattle: Alaska Northwest Books, 1986.

Canadian Hydrographic Service: *British Columbia Pilot, Vol I & II* . Ottawa, 1965

Craven, Margaret. *I Heard the Owl Call My Name*. New York: Doubleday,1972

Farwell, Captain R.F. *Captain Farwell's Hansen Handbook*. Seattle: L&H Printing, 1951.

Gibbs, Jim. *Disaster Log of Ships*. Seattle: Superior Publishing, 1971.

Goetzmann, William & Sloan, Kay, *Looking Far North, The Harriman Expedition to Alaska*, 1899, Princeton: Princeton Univ. Press, 1982.

Hill, Beth. *Upcoast Summers*. Ganges, British Columbia: Horsdal & Schubart, 1985.

Hoyt, Erich. *Orca: the Whale Named Killer*. Buffalo: Firefly Press, 1990.

Huntington, Sydney, *Shadows on the Koyukuk*, Seattle: Alaska Northwesst Books, 1993.

Iglauer, Edith. *Fishing With John*. New York: Farrar, Straus & Giroux, 1988.

Jackson, W.H. *Handloggers*. Anchorage: Alaska Northwest Publishing, 1974.

Janson, Lone, *The Copper Spike*, Anchorage: Alaska Northwest Books, 1973.

Jonaitis, Aldona, editor. *Chiefly Feasts*. Seattle: University of Washington Press, 1991.

Jonaitis, Aldona. *From the Land of the Totem Poles*. Seattle: Univ. of Washington Press, 1988.

Kent, Rockwell, *Wilderness*, New Haven: Leete's Island Books, 1975.

MacDonald, George, *Chiefs of the Land and Sky*, Vancouver: UBC Press, 1993.

Mckeown, Martha. *The Trail Led North*: *Mont Hawthorne's Story*. Portland, Oregon: Binfords & Mort, 1960.

Moore, Terris, *Mt. McKinley, The Pioneer Climbs*, Seattle: The Mountaineers, 1981.

Muir, John. *Travels in Alaska*. Boston: Houghton, Mifflin Co., 1915.

Murie, Margaret, *Two in the Far North*, Portland: Alaska Northwest Books, 1975.

Murie, Olaus, *Journeys to the Far North*, Palo Alto: The Wilderness Society, 1973.

Newell, Gordon and Joe Williamson. *Pacific Tugboats*. Seattle: Superior Publishing, 1957.

Nicholson, George. *Vancouver Island's West Coast*. Victoria, B. C.: Moriss Printing, 1965.

Ritter, Harry. *Alaska's History*. Portland: Alaska Northwest Books, 1993.

Rushton, Gerald. *Echoes of the Whistle*. Vancouver: Douglas & McIntyre, 1980.

Ryan, John J. *The Maggie Murphy*. New York: W.W. Norton & Co., 1951.

Sherwonit, Bill, *To The Top of Denali*, Seattle: Alaska Northwest Books, 1997.

U. S. Dept. of Commerce. *United States Coastal Pilot, Vol 8 & 9*. Washington, D.C. 1969.

Upton, Joe, *Alaska Blues*. Anchorage: Alaska Northwest Publishing, 1977.

Upton, Joe, *The Coastal Companion*, Bainbridge Island, WA: Coastal Publishing, 1995

Upton, Joe, *Journeys Through the Inside Passage*. Portland: Alaska Northwest Books, 1992.

Vancouver, George. *A Voyage of Discovery to the North Pacific Ocean and Round the World*, London, 1798.

Walbran, Captain John T. *British Columbia Coast Names*. Ottawa: Government Printing Bureau

Howward, editor. *Raincoast Chronicles: Forgotten Villages of the B.C. Coast*. Madeira Park: Harbour Publishing, 1987.

Index

Alaska place names:

Joe Upton
Fords Terror, Alaska, 2009

Traveling northwest waters as a commercial fisherman since 1965 in small craft and large, Joe Upton gained intimate knowledge of the coast from Puget Sound almost to the Arctic Circle.

In the 1970s Upton lived and fished out of a tiny island community in the roadless wilderness of Southeast Alaska. His first book, *Alaska Blues*, based on those years, was hailed as "One of those books you want to proclaim a classic" by the *Seattle Post Intelligencer*.

In 1995, Upton established Coastal Publishing to produce illustrated maps and guidebooks for Alaska cruise travelers.

Upton teamed up with film maker Dan Kowalski in 2009 to start making videos to accompany his books and maps.

Joe and Mary Lou Upton live on Bainbridge Island, WA.